"Then **Ozzie** Said to **Harold**..."

The Best Chicago White Sox Stories Ever Told

Lew Freedman and Billy Pierce

TRIUMPH
B O O K S

Triumph Books and colophon are registered trademarks of Random House, Inc.

Library of Congress Cataloging-in-Publication Data

Freedman, Lew, 1951–
"Then Ozzie said to Harold" : the best Chicago White Sox stories ever told / Lew Freedman and Billy Pierce
      p. cm.
   Includes bibliographical references.
   ISBN-13: 978-1-60078-063-9
   ISBN-10: 1-60078-063-6
1. Chicago White Sox (Baseball team)—History. 2. Chicago White Sox (Baseball team)—Anecdotes. I. Pierce, Billy, 1927– II. Title.
   GV875.C58F737 2008
   796.357'640977311—dc22
                                        2008000067

This book is available in quantity at special discounts for your group or organization. For further information, contact:

Triumph Books
542 South Dearborn Street
Suite 750
Chicago, Illinois 60605
(312) 939-3330
Fax (312) 663-3557

Printed in U.S.A.
ISBN: 978-1-60078-063-9
Design by Patricia Frey

Photo Credits:
All photos courtesy of Getty Images unless otherwise indicated.

*To my wife, Gloria, my family,
and all the loyal, great White Sox fans.*

—Billy Pierce

table of
contents

preface

Billy Pierce is one of the most popular players in Chicago White Sox history. The southpaw came to the South Side of Chicago in a trade with Detroit in 1949, and he was traded to the San Francisco Giants in 1962. But in a sense, he never left.

Pierce has resided in the Chicago area for about 45 years, and he has been as closely identified with the White Sox in retirement as he was as one of the signature players of the Go-Go White Sox of the 1950s. That refreshing group of players reversed the fortunes of an ailing franchise buried in the nether regions of the American League standings since the 1919 Black Sox Scandal. They carried the Sox to their first World Series appearance in 40 years and the only one between 1919 and 2005.

A slightly built, 5'10", 160-pound left-hander whose fastball packed surprising pop, Pierce won 211 games in his 18-year major league career, 186 of them for Chicago. Pierce twice won 20 games in a season, led the American League in earned-run average with a 1.97 mark in 1955, and pitched four one-hitters for the White Sox.

The White Sox retired his No. 19 jersey and erected a statue at U.S. Cellular Field commemorating his career. Pierce is fondly remembered by White Sox fans along with 1950s compatriots like Minnie Minoso, Nellie Fox, and Luis Aparicio. Theirs was a special era in White Sox history. But White Sox history predates all of their births, and the team had many successes on the diamond in the early part of the 20th century. Many of the greatest players in Sox lore are among the all-time greats of the game. Hall of Famers dotted the White Sox lineup in every decade. One of the pinnacles of franchise achievement occurred only recently when the club triumphed in the 2005 World Series, the first championship victory for the team since 1917.

Each era of White Sox play offers entertaining tales from the field, the clubhouse, and the ballpark. Whether the players wore flannels or double knits; whether the players are ghostly figures like Big Ed Walsh from the dead-ball era; more flesh-and-blood familiar like Red Faber, Ted Lyons, and Luke Appling; or modern-day baseball heroes like Paul Konerko or A.J. Pierzynski, they offer insights, emotions, and stories about what it was or what it is like to be a member of the Chicago White Sox.

—Lew Freedman

acknowledgments

Thank you to Chicago White Sox officials for all of their help, and thank you to current and former White Sox players for taking the time to talk about their playing days.

A special thank you goes to the National Baseball Hall of Fame Library, director Tim Wiles, and his staff.

introduction

I grew up in Detroit, so I signed with the Tigers. There was no draft in those days, but that was the home team, and I wanted to sign with the home team. I didn't pitch much in 1945, but at age 18, I ended up on a world-championship team. Some fellows play their whole career and don't get there.

Oh, my gracious, I was wide-eyed. We had Hal Newhouser, a 25-game winner, Dizzy Trout, and the great hitter Hank Greenberg, who came back from the service. There were some pretty fair ballplayers. My role, really, was just to be around to soak it up and learn. I pitched 10 innings that whole year.

My big game was in Boston at Fenway Park. I went into the game with the bases loaded, and when I was coming in from the bullpen in right field, the right fielder says, "Bill, don't get excited." Then the center fielder comes over and says, "Bill, take it easy." And the second baseman goes, "Bill, it's all right. Just go get them." The score was 4–1. I pitched for four innings and shut them out. We lost 4–3. Afterward, manager Steve O'Neill comes over, and he says, "Bill, I'm proud of you. You did a great job." I didn't pitch again for six weeks and got sent to Buffalo in the minors. I always wondered where I would be now if he hadn't been so proud of me.

I came back up, and we were in the World Series. It was a tremendous thrill. There's no question about it. I hurt my back in 1946 and didn't pitch much. I pitched in Buffalo in 1947, and I was back in Detroit in 1948 and didn't pitch much. In 1949 they were talking about how they were going to keep some of the young pitchers out of the bullpen—I was one of them—and it wasn't two weeks later I was traded to Chicago. I was at my wife Gloria's home before we were married, and I heard it from a disc jockey on the radio.

I never wanted to get traded to Chicago because it was dusty around Comiskey Park at night due to the proximity of the stock-yards. The aroma was terrible back in those days. It was brutal.

So, naturally, I got traded to Chicago. As it turned out, it was the biggest break I ever got because I got a chance to pitch. The White Sox had done nothing in 1948. They lost 101 ballgames, so they were giving everybody opportunities. That's what I mainly asked for, an opportunity to pitch. We had a lot of fellows coming and going. Frank Lane was the general manager. They called him Trader Lane. As it turned out, I was the first trade he made.

Then he traded for Chico Carrasquel and Nellie Fox. And Minnie Minoso came over from the Indians. Gradually, from 1949 to 1951, the team got better. I had a problem with my arm in 1954. The trainer gave me two aspirin and rubbed hot stuff on my arm. Then I went out there and threw it out. It happened again to me in 1955, so I only pitched every five or six days, but I ended up with a 1.97 earned-run average.

I lost four games 1–0, but I pitched well, which is the important thing. And in 1956 and 1957 the arm was great. I won 20 games both years. I could never have fun throwing the ball from the outfield again, though. I had to work out the stiffness first every time.

The 1950s were a fun time in White Sox baseball. The Go-Go White Sox started in '51, and we were always contenders until we finally made it to the World Series in 1959. The players were close. I was very friendly with Nellie Fox, Luis Aparicio, Jim Landis, Jim Rivera, and Minnie Minoso.

When I retired from baseball in 1964, we lived in Evergreen Park, a Chicago suburb. All my kids went through school there, and my wife and I moved to Lemont, another Chicago suburb, about 10 years ago. I stayed in touch with the White Sox, and the ownerships have all been fantastic to me over the years.

I was thrilled when the White Sox retired my No. 19 in 1987. The number is on the left-field wall with a picture of me. It was fantastic when the team did that. Not only for me, but for my three children and my grandchildren when they go out to the park. There used to be just a plaque out there in right field with each retired number, and now they put the pictures out there. The organization has been great to me.

I have been retired for 40 years now, and baseball has changed so much. The media promotes everything much more, and attendance is higher than it has ever been. You don't see kids playing on playgrounds as much, but there are still the Little Leagues and the Pony Leagues, and baseball is still kids' favorite game. To me it's still a wonderful game. It's still three strikes, three outs, four balls; that concept hasn't changed.

The ballparks have changed, though, and I think the new ballparks in baseball are beautiful. To me the new Sox park, U.S. Cellular Field, is the most beautiful thing. It's so clean and nice, and there are no poles in the way. I played in old Comiskey Park, and I loved it, but this ballpark is better, without question. When I go out to the park to watch the White Sox, I buy my two grilled hot dogs with a large Pepsi, the same as the other fans. That's my menu.

Baseball still has a hold on me, and I watch the White Sox all the time. Just think how happy I was in 2005 when they won the World Series. Owner Jerry Reinsdorf and the organization gave me a World Series ring. It's a great game. I watched my sons play ball, and I like to watch my grandchildren play. I like to watch all the sports.

The modern players are different than they used to be. They are bigger and stronger, but they are not always strong on the fundamentals. I saw a fellow in left field raise just one hand to catch the ball, and he dropped it. We were always taught to use two hands to catch the ball. Now it's nonchalant, one-handed, and I've seen more balls dropped than I ever saw while I played. A lot of fundamental things went by the wayside in light of the home run, which is a fan favorite.

Professionally, baseball has changed for pitchers. Now when a pitcher throws six innings and gives up three runs, they call it a "quality start." I hate to call it a quality start. That's an earned-run average of 4.50. The part that gets me is *quality*. When the White Sox won the World Series in 2005, they had four complete games in a row. So, I mean, it can still be done, and the same fellows who got relieved during the season went nine innings in the playoff games.

When Paul Richards managed the White Sox in the 1950s, I would pitch for one day. Then, in the middle of my days of rest, I would come in to relieve for a batter or an inning.

Now you don't see that at all. A starting pitcher takes his turn, and that's all there is to it. It was ridiculous when a tie was called in the All-Star Game a couple of years ago because they said the pitchers couldn't pitch anymore. I started three All-Star Games, and I pitched three innings in each one. That's how it was. You could use three pitchers for three innings apiece, and that was the game.

Now you have a seventh-inning pitcher, an eighth-inning pitcher, and a ninth-inning closer. We never heard of such a thing back then. If you couldn't start, you relieved. Long relievers could go five innings. It wasn't one inning or two innings.

I have no idea what my velocity was when I pitched. My fastball might have been somewhere in the 90s. I mean, you can't throw a ball by a hitter like Ted Williams or Joe DiMaggio if you're not throwing fairly fast. But they had no radar guns in those days. I watch fellows throwing now, and they say it's 95 mph, and I don't believe it. I watched Nolan Ryan, and when he was throwing that ball it was going fast. That fellow was throwing in the high 90s. A 93 mph fastball is fast, but hittable. The 98s and 100s are pretty much unhittable if you throw them in the right spots. You know what, though? Despite the changes, I still always pull for the pitcher.

—Billy Pierce

chapter 1

Dead-Ball White Sox

Charles Comiskey, pictured here as a member of the St. Louis Browns in the late 1880s, founded the Chicago White Sox when he moved the team from St. Paul, Minnesota.

Beginnings

The origin of the Chicago White Sox really dates back to a son's disobedience to his father, though like George Washington when he chopped down that eternal cherry tree, Charles Comiskey did not tell a lie.

Charles A. Comiskey was 17 years old in 1876 and on the job toting bricks across Chicago's West Side for a remodeling project at City Hall. His horse-drawn transport came upon a baseball game. He stopped to watch as pitchers from both teams were battered one after the other by hitters clouting safeties. He was heard to utter the phrase, "Gee, I can pitch better than that." As his load of bricks went unattended, a manager took Comiskey up on his boast.

Eventually the player's father, Honest John Comiskey, found him. Whatever career Dad had in mind for the young man died on that sandlot. Comiskey devoted himself to baseball after that. He became a masterful fielding first baseman for the St. Louis Browns, introducing innovative techniques around the bag and becoming the first to venture far from the foul line. Over time Comiskey emerged not only as a first-rate ballplayer over a 13-year major league career, but also as an astute businessman.

When Ban Johnson, commissioner of the Western League, changed the name to the American League for the 1901 season to compete against the National League's monopoly, Comiskey was operating the St. Paul, Minnesota, franchise. He asked to move the team to Chicago. Grudgingly, through political maneuvers, permission for the move was granted; but as part of the agreement Comiskey was bound not to construct a ballpark farther north than 35th Street, to avoid competition with the North Side Chicago Cubs. To this day the White Sox have never occupied a stadium farther north in Chicago. The team's modern home, U.S. Cellular Field, is located at 35th and Shields Avenue, across the street from the original 1910 Comiskey Park that the owner built.

Comiskey was the first ballplayer to morph into an owner. At various times during his tenure as boss of the White Sox—until his death in 1931—Comiskey was regarded as a cheapskate by his players. But he was appreciated by newspaper reporters as sociable, friendly, and a guy willing to pick up the tab. Comiskey was nicknamed the Old Roman. It was a term of affection and respect, not a derogatory appellation, as if he was Nero fiddling while Rome burned. That viewpoint was ascribed to him later, during the infamous Black Sox Scandal of 1919.

Somehow, for most of his baseball career, Comiskey obscured his age. As he got older and his playing days receded in the rearview mirror, Comiskey pretended to be six years younger. In 1913, at a party, he revealed that he had really been born on August 15, 1858. It was part of Comiskey's schtick to say that he had a birthday every day. That left his listeners laughing and confused enough to preserve his secret. At least once he publicly denied that he celebrated his birthday twice a year.

In 1913, at a splashy gathering where city, state, and national officials were present to honor Comiskey for his service to baseball, he was presented with a new collection of office furniture. Comiskey joked that the new furniture was so fancy he would no longer sign players' contracts in his office because they would think it was so plush he could afford to pay them more.

Reporters who heard Comiskey announce his birth date were skeptical. So were researchers in later years. The *Baseball Encyclopedia* does grant August 15 as Comiskey's birthday, but says he was born in 1859.

Comiskey was a party animal, but he most assuredly had a competitive side. A story recounted in the book *The Chicago White Sox,* written by longtime Chicago journalist Warren Brown, indicates that Comiskey once lost his temper over a lobster.

Comiskey had ordered lobster at a prime Chicago restaurant, and he was the charming host of a small gathering until his dish arrived. Staring at the lobster on his plate, Comiskey was disappointed to see a claw broken partially off. He asked the waiter how the damage happened. The thinking-on-his-feet server replied that lobsters in the wild sometimes break their claws while fighting.

Mustering the type of wrath more suited to learning that his star pitcher might have suffered a broken wing, Comiskey yelled, "Then take the damn thing away and bring me the winner!"

Hitless Wonders

Rarely has a major league team been so bad on paper and won so handily on the field as the Chicago White Sox of 1906. During the dead-ball era of baseball—pre–Babe Ruth and the 1920s—teams hit few home runs. Offense was built around advancing a base at a time, scratching out one run at a time. A typical run might be scored on a bunt single, a stolen base, the runner going to third on a ground-out to second and coming home on an error.

Baseballs were not so tightly wound and, unlike in the modern game, were not replaced by umpires for the slightest scuff mark. In baseball's early days, fans were expected to throw back foul balls, not keep them as souvenirs. Except for ballparks where it has become chic to throw a visiting player's home-run ball back onto the field, such a notion seems quaint. The political fallout of ushers wrestling wide-eyed little boys for the balls their dads caught would not be a pretty picture. Decades ago fans returned the balls willingly, and they were often used in play until they became soft and lopsided. Advantage pitcher, disadvantage power hitter.

Yet even by the mild hitting standards of the day, the 1906 White Sox could barely hit their way out of the infield. Still, they finished the regular season 93–58, won the American League pennant, then upset the crosstown Chicago Cubs, winners of a record 116 games, in the World Series. Frank Isbell hit .279, the club's best average, and as a team the Sox hit an anemic .230. It was the lowest batting average ever for a pennant winner. On their run to glory, the inexplicable White Sox won 19 games in a row, also a record.

With their 116–36 record, the Cubs expected to roll over the White Sox in what at the time was called the Trolley Car Series.

Many Hall of Famers competed, including the Cubs' famed double-play combination—Joe Tinker, Johnny Evers, and Frank Chance—and immortal pitcher Mordecai "Three Finger" Brown. The Sox countered with Big Ed Walsh, Doc White, and timelier hitting to win the Series 4–2. Although there were several well-pitched games, Walsh's two-hitter with 12 strikeouts in a 3–0 Game 3 victory was pivotal. The Sox were without injured regular shortstop George Davis, too. Somehow the Hitless Wonders delivered a championship while batting just .198 for the Series, thus living up to their nickname.

The pitcher who helped the White Sox set the tone in the opener was left-hander Nick Altrock, one of baseball's great characters. Altrock, who made his major league debut in 1898 and played through 1924, was the 2–1 victor over the Cubs in the first game. A brief portion of Altrock's career was exceptional when he won 19, 20, and 23 games for the Sox in 1904, 1905, and 1906, respectively. But after becoming a vaudeville-type overnight sensation in the coaching box, Altrock converted to a fielder to better take advantage of playing opportunities.

Otherwise Altrock was known as a baseball funnyman whose clowning on the diamond provided more fan satisfaction than his attempts to locate the strike zone. Altrock possessed an expressive face, and he employed it energetically while dispensing his comedy. He was once described thus: "He has palm-leaf ears projecting like propellers. His nose reminds one of an inflated hot dog and his pachydermatous countenance of a dried elephant's pelt." The general interpretation would be that Altrock had big ears and a rubbery face. Altrock was the Clown Prince of Baseball before Max Patkin inherited the title.

Altrock, who performed at ballparks for decades, found that fans booed his humor more than his fastball. Once he tried to silence a fan by knocking his ears with debate. "If I had your mouth full of dollars bills, I'd retire," Altrock said. "If I had your ears full of nickels, I'd retire," the fan retaliated. Altrock merely laughed and said, "I guess the fan was right, but I wouldn't trade them ears for his mouth. Not even with the world's greatest tenderloin steak thrown in. Why, them ears are my trademark."

Sometimes Altrock teamed up with Al Schacht, a pitcher who had a brief fling with the Washington Senators between 1919 and 1921, and who also had a better sense of humor than control. Altrock introduced himself to Schacht by making fun of the other player's oversized nose. "Is that your schnozzle, or are you eating a banana?" Altrock asked. A beautiful partnership was born. For a time Altrock and Schacht reenacted the Jack Dempsey–Luis Firpo heavyweight championship bout. Dempsey won by knockout. The imitative duo always pulled their punches until the day Schacht thought it might improve the act if he connected on the KO bomb. This time when Altrock's facial muscles proved as flexible as silly putty, it was the real deal.

Altrock enjoyed playing golf, but he didn't have the ready cash for membership at the finest country clubs. He sometimes used his well-known, easily recognizable face as a calling card. Once Altrock was on an excursion in the Deep South and felt the itch to play the local links. He rented a limousine and directed it to a private club. Altrock unloaded his clubs and tipped a servant to carry the bag into the clubhouse. He hung around a moment or two until a group noticed him and, sure enough, one player recognized him. "Don't you gentlemen know that guy?" the player asked. "Why, he's Nick Altrock."

The golfers flipped a coin for the right to include Altrock in their foursome.

Spitball Man

Before every mother admonished her son for spitting in public, Big Ed Walsh buttered his bread with saliva, so to speak. The greatest pitcher in Chicago White Sox history relied less on a fastball and curveball than on the spitter, which was legal to use during his early-20th-century career.

Shown here in 1915, Ed Walsh was a master of the spitball and advocated throughout his life for its return to professional baseball.

Walsh is a mythical figure in White Sox history. Although he led a long life, he is little-known to Sox fans of today except through the astounding numbers next to his name in the record books. Walsh was born in Pennsylvania in 1881 and died in Florida 78 years later. He stood 6'1" in his prime, tall for the early 1900s. Except for four appearances in his final season of 1917, Walsh pitched entirely for the White Sox starting in 1904. His career record was 195–126.

Reviewing some of Walsh's individual season totals leaves observers openmouthed. In 1908 Walsh won 40 games with a 1.42 earned-run average while throwing 464 innings and completing 42 of the 49 games he started. That was only the third-best ERA of Walsh's career, and four other times he threw between 368 and 422 innings in a season. You could almost hear Walsh saying, "I don't need no stinking relief pitchers." He was more of a workhorse than a Budweiser Clydesdale.

A modern manager who allowed a pitcher to throw that many innings would be arrested, ordered to repent, and sent to a reeducation camp in Afghanistan, probably for good reason. Walsh's spectacular career was cut short by arm miseries. His right arm probably dangled six inches longer than his left by the time he retired. In a career switch unfathomable to most baseball people, Walsh actually became a big-league umpire for a season in 1922. He also coached for the White Sox during their lean years in the 1920s.

For decades the debate raged over who was the best player that ever lived—Ty Cobb or Babe Ruth. But Walsh never hesitated in picking the 4,000-hit man over the 700–home run man. Not that he conceded much to the old Detroit Tiger, either.

"I never had any trouble with Ty," Walsh said. "He'd hit me. I'd stop him. He was the greatest. Ruth was a great pitcher when he was in it. Hitting the home runs, he had it. But the greatest was Mr. Ty Cobb. That's Mister Baseball for me."

Throughout his life, Walsh, who estimated that he signed 1.5 million autographs—more than Paris Hilton, Jessica Simpson, and Britney Spears combined—advocated for the return of the banned spitball to the sport he loved. It was no surprise that he admired the play of master strategist Cobb more than that of smash-'em-over-the-wall Ruth. Walsh was a product of the dead-ball era, and the way the game should be played was fixed in his mind from his youth and was never dislodged as power hitters took over the sport.

"The ball is too lively," Walsh, who never lived to hear of steroids, said in the early 1950s. "Everybody can hit a home run now. Why, I remember in '06 when we had a team batting average of .225 [actually .230] we had only three home runs all season [actually five], and I hit one of them. And to top it off, they took away from the pitcher a great pitch, the spitter.

"Unsanitary, my foot. You didn't slobber on the ball. Elmer Stricklett, the father of the spitball, taught it to me when we were rookie teammates in Chicago [in 1904], and I got it so I could break it different ways—straight down, down and away, or in—and if I came underhanded I could move it up-and-in on a hitter, too. Yet I barely wet two fingers before gripping the ball."

Walsh thought baseball was conspiring against pitchers even making a living because of the popularity of the home run.

"Livelier baseballs, smaller ballparks," he said. "They've practically got the poor pitchers working in straight jackets. They say removing the spitter cuts down on hit batsmen. Bah! They still allow the knuckleball, and that's three times as hard to control as the spitter."

In 1958, with Walsh in a wheelchair and suffering from arthritis and cancer, the White Sox toasted him with a special day at Comiskey Park. At the end of the Ed Walsh Day ceremony, Walsh spoke and said, "This day I'll remember as long as I live."

Then Walsh prepared to toss out a ceremonial first pitch to his old catcher, Ray Schalk, another Hall of Famer. "Throw him a spitball, Ed," someone teased Walsh. The idea tickled Walsh, and his face lit up. Then Walsh licked two fingers, gripped the ball, and threw to Schalk. The "pitch" traveled only about five feet into Schalk's mitt, but the old man made his point.

chapter 2
Prosperity and Scandal

A team photo of the 1919 White Sox—the team responsible for the Black Sox Scandal, the biggest scandal in baseball history. Shoeless Joe Jackson is dead center in the bottom row.

Around the World

Travel was a bit slower in November 1913 when the Chicago White Sox and the New York Giants embarked on an around-the-world mission to spread the good word about baseball to unsuspecting nations that didn't know the hit-and-run from ring-around-the-rosy. It was a plan hatched by Comiskey and Giants manager John McGraw, and in an era without air travel, they traveled by ship to numerous exotic ports of call.

Actually, the players were not all Giants or White Sox, but representatives from many teams under the umbrella of those two clubs. The most notably misassigned player was young pitcher Red Faber, a White Sox minor leaguer who soon blossomed into a Hall of Famer. Farber was lent to the Giants for the duration before playing a single major league game for the Sox.

From a worldwide standpoint, the most famous player in the group was Jim Thorpe. Few people outside the United States knew anything about baseball, but Thorpe was at the peak of his fame. He had won the gold medal in the decathlon in the 1912 Summer Olympics and was heralded as the greatest athlete in the world. Although the term *Native American* was not in vogue at the time, when Comiskey welcomed Thorpe to the troupe, he said, "Why not? He's the only real American in the party, isn't he?"

The Americans sailed across the Pacific Ocean from Vancouver, Canada, and first played in Japan. They proceeded to China, the Philippines, and on to Australia, competing in three cities on that continent. Sometimes the touring major leaguers played head-to-head with indigenous clubs. But any baseball played overseas in 1913 was a far cry from the quality exhibited when teams from Japan and Cuba, most notably, pursued Olympic gold medals nearly a century later. The locals took beatings of 10–1 and 18–0 from the Giants and Sox in Australia. G'day, mate.

A most humorous exchange occurred in Egypt when the traveling teams played in Cairo before the royal head of state, Abbas Hilmi II, the *khedive* of Egypt. The leader brought his 43 wives to the game along with their 100 servants. Talk about filling a skybox.

During the game the White Sox pulled off a rare triple play. The spectacular occurrence drew no special appreciation from the head guy, however, most likely because he didn't really gather its significance. Still, Norris "Tip" O'Neill, one of Comiskey's assistants (he traveled with fewer than 100 servants), seemed miffed and took the lack of demonstrative reaction as a slight.

"He didn't even notice that triple play!" O'Neill said to Comiskey.

Comiskey gazed at his man and said, "He's got enough to do. If you had 43 wives to watch, you wouldn't notice a triple play, either."

Piling on the mileage, even if no frequent-traveler points were earned, the teams played in Italy—where the group met Pope Pius X—and France before moving on to England in late February, 1914, three full months into the extraordinary swing. This brought the Americans to the home of cricket and the 16th-century game, rounders. Over the course of subsequent investigation, some historians thought baseball's origins stemmed from those games. It seemed likely the ballplayers performed before a more understanding audience—an audience that included King George V. Comiskey and Chicago sportswriter Joe Farrell sat in the king's box and quietly explained various nuances of the game to His Royal Majesty. It was a close game with several tight calls, and Farrell later reported that the king said little when he told him what was going on. When a key catch was made in foul territory and the king turned to Farrell to say, "A most useful catch, wasn't it?", the writer wondered if the king didn't know a whole lot more about baseball than he let on.

The game attracted 30,000 fans, who drank in the scene and watched with bemusement, if not significant comprehension. The British press was out in force, as well, and reported in a style that would amuse the American readers. The narrow conclusion: baseball would never replace cricket in England's heart.

One newspaper report in a London newspaper said the sport was definitely "glorified rounders," though dramatically developed. "It is superbly organized and specialized in every detail; but the framework of the old English game still remains. Secondly, in batting, in spite of all the gorgeous smiting that was seen, baseball does not compare with cricket. Next, the cleverness and the velocity of the pitching are wonderful. Finally, there is no fielding in cricket which approaches the fielding and throwing which were seen yesterday."

Red Faber, Spitball Man II

It figured that a man whose real first name was Urban played baseball for a big-city team. Urban Faber had one of the best pitching careers in the history of the White Sox but played so long ago that few current-day fans recall his exploits. There were many of them.

Faber, from Dubuque, Iowa, so favorably impressed John McGraw while on loan during the world tour that the Giants' mentor offered Comiskey $50,000 for his contract. Comiskey figured that if McGraw knew his talent, he would keep Faber—and he never regretted it. Faber won 254 major league games, all with the White Sox, including more than 20 in a season four times, and was one of the last legal spitballers grandfathered in after the pitch was outlawed in 1920.

Faber was 16 when he made his debut for his hometown Dubuque semipro team, collecting $2 a game, but he didn't break into the majors until he was 25. Maybe it was fate, but Faber was the key performer a few seasons into his major league career when the White Sox met the Giants in the 1917 World Series.

A friend from Iowa remarked that Faber looked cool and calm in the intense championship atmosphere, but Faber said that was a good masquerade. "Maybe it seemed that way," he said. "Maybe I didn't show it, but I was praying before every pitch." Somebody up there heard his entreaties, or else Faber's baffling spitball was simply enough to bamboozle the Giants hitters, but he won three games in the only Series the White Sox won between 1917 and 2005.

Urban "Red" Faber, shown here warming up before a game, enjoyed one of the longest and best White Sox careers in history.

The redheaded Faber was the pivotal player in the victory, but the White Sox were a very solid club all-around, featuring stars like Shoeless Joe Jackson, Ed Cicotte, Eddie Collins, and Buck Weaver. It is little-remembered by comparison to the 1919 pennant winners accused of throwing the World Series to Cincinnati that the 1917 team was populated by most of the same players, and they were regarded as one of the best teams of all time.

Faber was the hero of the Series, but he also committed a well-remembered gaffe running the bases against the Giants that provoked major league laughter at the time. In Game 2, with two outs, Faber reached base in the fifth inning on a single and advanced to second on a throw to the plate. He was positive the runner ahead of him, Buck Weaver, had scored. Faber decided to take advantage of the pitcher's slow windup and dashed for third, certain he had the base stolen cleanly.

One problem: Weaver was already there. Giants third baseman Heinie Zimmerman took the throw and tagged both Weaver and Faber. Faber was the one called out for the third out of the Sox inning. A steaming Weaver asked, "Where the hell are you going?" Faber replied, "I'm goin' to pitch."

It was not long, however, before spectators were laughing or fuming at Zimmerman, accused of making one of the most vivid mistakes in World Series lore. The White Sox took a 3–0 lead in the fourth inning of the sixth and final game after Collins outran Zimmerman to the plate. Runners were on first and third, and the Giants infield was at double-play depth, seeking to cut off Collins at home. Sox center fielder Happy Felsch hit the ball back to the mound, and Collins feinted off third, hoping to confuse the New York infielders and disrupt the double play.

Suddenly Collins sprinted toward the plate. The logical play was for Zimmerman to throw the ball home to easily cut off the runner. But Giants catcher Bill Rariden was nowhere to be found. Zimmerman took off in hot pursuit like a police officer chasing a thief. He did not throw home, and Collins outran him and scored a critical run. Rariden had run the first-base line, so Zimmerman had no target. Yet it was Zimmerman who was blamed as the fall guy on the play, and the label of *goat* followed him throughout his life. Sometimes he angrily retorted that he had to give chase because there was nobody to throw to in the vicinity of home plate except the umpire—and that guy wasn't taking sides.

Later the White Sox honored the pitcher with a special day. Red Faber Day occurred in 1929, and there it was announced, "Urban Faber is my ideal of all a baseball player should be. He is an example for all American youth to follow." Faber pitched against home-run slugger Babe Ruth many times during his years with the Red Sox and Yankees, but Ruth later described the hurler as "the nicest man in the world."

The White Sox were definitely the best baseball team in the world in 1917, and manager Clarence "Pants" Rowland was particularly proud of it. In an era when player-managers were common and when stars typically ascended to take the reins of major league clubs, Rowland had never played big-league ball. He had trouble winning the respect of the snootier players who whispered that he was a bush leaguer.

Decades later, when the White Sox were poised to win the 1959 pennant, Rowland was an 80-year-old vice president of the Chicago Cubs. He was still sticking up for his boys. "I've never seen a team as good as that 1917 outfit," Rowland said. "No Yankees team, no Athletics team, no team."

The White Sox of 1959 had strength up the middle, leaning on All-Stars Luis Aparicio at shortstop and Nellie Fox at second base, but Rowland conceded nothing. Neither would have been able to beat out Buck Weaver, Swede Risberg, Eddie Collins, or Chick Gandil in his locked-in infield, he felt.

"Nobody could have cracked that infield," Rowland said. "It was the best, even though, and when, some of them turned out to be crooks."

That they did.

The Black Sox Scandal

It was as if Charles Dickens had written his famous line from *A Tale of Two Cities*—"It was the best of times, it was the worst of times"—for the 1919 White Sox. The Sox were the dominant American League team, and they blitzed to the pennant. They were also heavily favored to win the World Series over the Cincinnati Reds.

It was considered a major upset when the White Sox fell to the Reds, but the shock was enhanced by the spreading dismay and gloom resulting from discussions at the ballparks and on the streets to the effect that the team had been ripe for gamblers and had thrown the World Series. Losing on purpose is the ultimate disgrace in competitive sports. To accept bribes to intentionally lose baseball's greatest prize left fans holding their noses from the stench, washing their mouths out from the sour taste, and embittered by the disdain shown by their diamond heroes.

The story of the Black Sox Scandal—and it is dirty laundry that could not be cleansed for years and that still hovers by name over the game—has been told and retold in newspapers, magazines, books, and movies. There were lies and double crosses, true confessions and disappearing confessions. So many variations of the "truth" have been explained that there is no way to ever know what actually happened. Who participated in the scam, and how much did everyone make? Those remain legitimate questions today. When did Charles Comiskey know, who told him, and how much did he know before the games were finished? No one's sure.

In the end, eight men were thrown out of baseball by new commissioner Kenesaw Mountain Landis in 1921 despite their acquittal by a Cook County court in Chicago. Of the group, the two men who complained the loudest about justice being ill-served were the great hitter Shoeless Joe Jackson, the outstanding tragic figure from the episode, and third baseman Buck Weaver, who spent decades trying to clear his name and gain reinstatement to baseball—even in old age. Famous baseball figures still are trying to earn Jackson, who died in 1951, reinstatement so he can be considered for the Hall of Fame.

Most of the others—Ed Cicotte, Swede Risberg, Chick Gandil, Felsch, Claude Williams, and Fred McMullin—faded into the woodwork. They went on about their lives away from their game almost as ghosts, and when sought out or encountered, they rarely spoke about the World Series of 1919. The most intriguing of that bunch was pitcher Cicotte. Cicotte was the key man bought by the gamblers and possibly the only one who made substantial money from the boondoggle despite many promises. Apparently Cicotte walked into retirement with $10,000. The entire scheme hinged on Cicotte's participation because he was the ace pitcher.

Cicotte was amenable to the fix because he was furious with Comiskey. During the 1919 regular season, Cicotte won 29 games.

He had a clause in his contract that if he won 30, Comiskey would fork over a bonus. But abruptly, as Cicotte seemed poised to capture his 30th win, he was removed from the rotation and never given the chance to throw for it. He felt he had been cheated out of the bonus.

Few baseball fans today remember Cicotte as anything other than a Black Sox fixer who was sent into exile with his brothers in crime. But if he hadn't been derailed by this huge lapse in judgment, Cicotte was probably on the path of accumulating the numbers needed for Hall of Fame acceptance.

In his 14 seasons, Cicotte, a 5'9", 175-pound right-hander, won 208 games and lost 149. His career earned-run average was a sparking 2.38. In his best season, 1917, Cicotte led the American League with a 1.53 ERA, and he came close to that a few other times. Nicknamed Knuckles, Cicotte is credited as the pitcher who perfected the knuckleball.

In a newspaper story at the end of the 1919 season, before the Series fix was uncovered, a headline read, "Cicotte Bares Pitching Secrets—as Far as He Says He Has Any." The story was accompanied by graphics showing Cicotte's grip on the ball and the different manners in which he could make it drop.

"Everybody knows that Cicotte for several years has kept in baseball by using some sort of trick delivery," the story read. "Everybody but Eddie himself, who won't admit it."

Decades later, Cicotte, who died in 1969, was interviewed by a Detroit sportswriter and said he had led an exemplary life ever since the scandal, without ever crossing the law again.

In an anonymous interview with New York sportswriter Joe Williams in the 1930s, a figure involved in the World Series deal waxed eloquent about different roles. The mysterious man, described only as "the little, middle-aged man," fingered gambling chieftain Arnold Rothstein as the mastermind. He said Cicotte did take the bucks and agreed to officially show the fix was on by hitting Cincinnati's first batter. This barroom interviewee also said Buck Weaver was clean all the way.

"I'm particularly sorry they kicked Buck Weaver out of the game," the talker said. "The kid didn't get a dime out of it, and he didn't know what was going on, either."

The interviewee said it would make interesting reading if the real story ever came out, but he wasn't going to tell it. Instead, as he informed Williams, he sat back and listened with amusement to the alternative, untrue tales that were circulating.

"It's funny some of the stuff you hear and read about what happened," the man said, "and what was to happen, about who did this, and who did that. Yes, it certainly is."

Whatever went down, it has been theorized many times that there never would have been a World Series fix by the White Sox if reliable pitcher Red Faber had been healthy enough to take his turn to pitch. Faber, with his three Series games in the bank in 1917 was seen as an above-reproach member of the "honest" block of the Sox, which also included Collins and catcher Ray Schalk. If Faber had been throwing at his best, it was said, the Sox would have prevailed and history would have been rewritten.

chapter 3

Roaring '20s and Depressing '30s

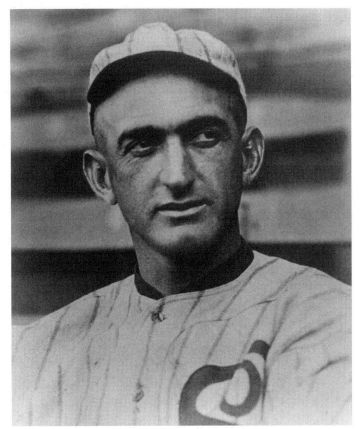

Shoeless Joe Jackson, expelled from baseball in 1919 for his supposed involvement in the Black Sox Scandal, always yearned to be back in the big leagues.

Shoeless Joe Never Forgets

Possessed of a stunning batting eye and dazzling coordination, Shoeless Joe Jackson was one of the greatest hitters of all time. From the time he was expelled from the game by commissioner Kenesaw Landis, until his death in 1951, Jackson professed innocence of any involvement in the fix.

Banned not only from the majors, but all of organized baseball, the exiled White Sox could not even suit up for pay in the minors, something Jackson would surely have done since he continued playing baseball on the sly. Often he played under an assumed name in semipro leagues, retaining his joy for the game but harboring bitterness about his circumstance. It was said that on one of his stopovers in Waycross, Georgia, he hit .535 in 100 games one summer, an astounding percentage even if Jackson was batting against toddlers.

Jackson was illiterate, and his employment prospects were not overwhelming once the thing he did best was taken from him. He was portrayed by newspapermen as a man easily led by shifty players on the team who wanted him to participate because of his ability to easily wreck their plans with his talent for the game. Similarly, his naïveté was played up when he showed up at the Cook County Courthouse to issue a confession—the one that mysteriously disappeared before trial.

Jackson owned one of the most enduring and memorable baseball nicknames of all time. There are various versions of how he came to be called *Shoeless*, but it is clear that he did not regularly play in the majors or elsewhere without baseball spikes or shoes. In an ancient interview, even before Jackson was transferred from the Cleveland Indians to the White Sox in 1915, Jackson expressed a yearning for retirement, a desire to set up his own farm. In that same discussion, he offered his story about how he was bestowed with the moniker *Shoeless*.

"I was playing in Anderson, South Carolina, one day," Jackson recounted, "and it happened that I played the day before in a new pair of baseball shoes. You know how ill-fitting shoes will act at times. Well, this pair simply raised the biggest blister you can imagine on each heel. So when I put on the shoes for the Anderson game I found I could hardly walk with them on, much less play ball. So the only thing for me to do was to take 'em off or die standing up—so I just naturally took 'em off and played in my stocking feet."

Such a move did not pass unnoticed, and a strong-voiced fan observed Jackson's sterling play and shouted, "Oh, you shoeless wonder."

Jackson said that's how his nickname stuck.

It remains difficult to know just what to make of Jackson's complicity in the sports crime of the century. Was he truly duped into taking the money, yet still played his best? Many investigators of the record conclude that he has paid his penance and should be reinstated into the sport, and with his lifetime .356 batting average, he should be considered on the Hall of Fame ballot.

Many times over the years as Jackson aged in South Carolina, reporters sought him out, always hoping for the exclusive true story. They generally went away dissatisfied, though some gleaned more than others. Jackson did not admit wrongdoing. Rather he took up the argument popularly being used in public by his supporters.

"I set more records in that World Series than any one man," Jackson told Chicago sportswriter John Carmichael. "And they ran me out of baseball. I never played in a league I didn't lead or on a club I didn't top. I got a lifetime average of almost .360, and I never shirked, never did anything but play my best. Maybe I ran with the wrong players. Maybe I heard things. But I tried to clear up the mess before it broke, and nobody listened. I went to Mr. Comiskey three weeks before the Series. I asked him to pull the team out; told him what I heard. He laughed and said, 'We got 100 men on guard...nothing could be pulled.' Then I asked him to let me withdraw. Suspend me or anything. And you know what he said? He said, 'Joe, it wouldn't be my team without you.'"

For all of its terrible consequences and poisoning of fan faith, the Black Sox Scandal is remembered best for the pithy phrase attributed to Jackson as he walked from court into a crowd.

According to lore, a little boy grabbed Jackson's sleeve and said, "Say it ain't so, Joe." Jackson supposedly bowed his head and said, "It's so."

It is unclear if Jackson ever uttered the words, and he may only have been admitting that the scam occurred, not his guilt, but the scene stuck to him better than superglue. When he died of a heart attack at age 62 in Greenville, South Carolina, Jackson was not operating the farm of his dreams; he was running a liquor store.

A Lion on the Mound

The Black Sox Scandal decimated the White Sox. Sometimes it seemed that South Side fans didn't smile from 1917 to 1940. The ejection of eight top players from the bunch that fixed the 1919 World Series fixed the White Sox but good for years, as owner Charles Comiskey tried to rebuild.

Between 1921, when Commissioner Landis sent the bad boys into permanent exile, and 1935, the White Sox never finished higher than fifth in the American League. They were as dismal as the Depression, as depressing as the early 1960s New York Mets.

The baseball world, with newfound hero Babe Ruth leading the way with his slugging prowess, pretty much passed the White Sox by during the 1920s. Ruth, heavyweight Jack Dempsey, flappers, and partying were all the rage of the decade. The White Sox still wore muddy socks. Pretty much the only good news during the entire decade was the unlikely arrival of a good-humored discovery named Ted Lyons in 1923.

Lyons attended Baylor University in Texas and, while intending to study law, joined the band to play trombone. Reportedly the bandleader suggested that he stick to baseball. Near the end of Lyons's college career a couple of Sox players in Texas volunteered to help out the team during spring training. As soon as they saw Lyons's right-handed stuff, they—especially catcher Ray Schalk—convinced the parent club to sign him. It was a good deal.

Hall of Famer Ted Lyons was a shining star during the most dismal period in White Sox history.

Lyons, nicknamed "Professor" because he was a college man, won a team-record 260 games in 21 seasons and was voted into the Hall of Fame. It was Lyons's misfortune, however, to be stuck in the White Sox dugout for the longest period of ghastly seasons in club history. It was Lyons's curse to become a big-time winner on a big-time loser, though he suffered alongside his teammates, also losing a team-record 230 games. At his most remarkable, Lyons won 22 games for the seventh-place 1930 White Sox. When he was 38, Lyons pitched 42 innings in a row without allowing a walk.

"If I were managing a team in an important game on which the pennant hinged," said star center fielder Tris Speaker, "and could pick any pitcher in baseball to pitch it, my choice would be Lyons. He can be as tough as anybody I know."

Lyons gained sympathy by starring for the Sox when they were perennial losers, and when he volunteered to join the Marines in 1942, just after the start of World War II, one wag suggested he was taking the easier assignment: "Old Ted's been paroled. They're giving him time off for good behavior."

The 1925 season typified Lyons's White Sox luck. He was good enough to win 21 games for a fifth-place squad, but he lost a no-hitter against the Washington Senators on a ninth-inning single. He did pitch a no-hitter in 1926. One reason Lyons was so popular with White Sox fans was that he stuck out the trying times for years without moaning. Lyons was never known to complain about his lot during this period—a period when players were bound to teams in perpetuity rather than being able to play out their options and become free agents. He gained the admiration of his peers for the way he hung in.

Luke Appling, the Hall of Fame shortstop who joined Lyons as one of the few Sox pluses said, "I never heard Ted complain. What a grand person he was. He had a heart as big as the Stone Mountain. I am certainly glad I was there to know him."

Lyons had to be a bulldog to endure the vagaries of a bad team for so long, but anyone who thought his generally pleasant demeanor meant that he did not care about winning and losing was definitely mistaken. He had a competitive temperament when he went to the mound, though he usually hid it on days off.

Chuck Comiskey, one of the family successors in ownership to Charles A., praised Lyons heartily as the most considerate and thoughtful person he ever met in his life. "Except on the day he pitched," Comiskey said. "He wouldn't shave, and when he came into the clubhouse everybody gave him all the room he wanted. He was a ferocious competitor. If a player made an error behind him, [that player'd] hear about it."

Lyons had every intention of pitching for the White Sox as long as his arm held out. As he moved into his fifth decade, he said, "Life begins at 40." War also began. Lyons briefly rejoined the Sox roster in 1945 before retiring, but then became team manager. He really liked those white socks.

More Stars Than the Night Sky

From the time the White Sox "contested" the 1919 World Series and famous sportswriter Ring Lardner walked through a frowning crowd of players singing, "I'm Forever Blowing Ballgames" to the tune of "I'm Forever Blowing Bubbles," the White Sox had not played in an important game.

There also seemed little likelihood of a change in fortunes any time soon when *Chicago Tribune* sports editor Arch Ward, who had as much P.T. Barnum coursing through his veins as Ernest Hemingway, dreamed up an alternative showcase to the World Series. Ward thought it would be a fine thing to create an All-Star Game. And the first one was scheduled to take place at Comiskey Park in 1933.

Ward's brilliant selling point was to hold a once-in-a-lifetime baseball game in conjunction with the Century of Progress World's Fair. There was never any thought by either Ward or baseball officials that the All-Star Game would become a permanent centerpiece of the baseball season. Using his own column to promote his idea, Ward termed the invention the Game of the Century.

It did not take long for the proposal to germinate into full bloom. Scheduled for July 6, the game prompted enthusiasm from team owners, players, and fans, and all wanted to be present. When 2,250 bleacher tickets went on sale two days prior to the game, they sold out in 45 minutes. "There will be no more tickets on sale before the game," Ward wrote. "That's all there is. There isn't any more."

The lineups for each side were impressive, with many future Hall of Famers lending their skills to the competition. Among the American League players were Babe Ruth, Lou Gehrig, Lefty Grove, Eddie Collins, Charlie Gehringer, Al Simmons, Lefty Gomez, and Bill Dickey. Among the National League players were Bill Terry, Hack Wilson, Carl Hubbell, Paul Waner, Gabby Hartnett, and Frankie Frisch.

Of the 36 players on the teams, 20 advanced to the Hall of Fame after it was created later in the decade. As always, there were stars among stars. Bill Hallahan, a National League pitcher for the St. Louis Cardinals, started the game and gave up a home run to Ruth.

"We wanted to see the Babe," Hallahan said after being taken to the cleaners. "Sure he was old and had a big waistline, but that didn't make any difference. We were on the same field as Babe Ruth."

Ward never could have envisioned the enduring popularity of the All-Star Game, and when the show returned to Comiskey Park in 1983 for the 50th anniversary of its debut, baseball officials estimated that 60 million people around the world watched it on television or listened on the radio.

Over the years baseball has amended, altered, shifted, and changed the rules for selection to the annual summer All-Star teams. These changes have prompted complaints about selection methods—about choosing players who were famous, but whose careers are on the downslide, over more deserving players of the moment. Yet it should be noted that fan votes were the key components in choosing the first teams.

Bucketfoot Al

Bucketfoot was not the most flattering nickname in the world, but it accurately described the awkward batting stance of Aloysius Simmons, generally known as Al. The right-handed-swinging Simmons stood in the batter's box with his left foot pointed almost straight down the third-base line. Fans and opposing players alike laughed at the sight and teased him, but they usually shut up when Simmons put on his devastating hitting exhibitions. Simmons batted .334 for his career, and no one made fun of that.

Connie Mack, Simmons's first professional manager, refused to be swayed by the guffaws because he believed in Simmons.

"Leave the young man alone," Mack said.

Simmons is most closely associated with the Philadelphia Athletics, but the hard-hitting outfielder played three productive seasons with the White Sox in 1933, 1934, and 1935, when they were about at their worst.

Of Polish descent with a given last name of Szymanski, Simmons grew up in Wisconsin and always had a soft spot for his minor league stay in Milwaukee. He was well aware that people ridiculed his stance, though he always had the last laugh with his slugging.

"Of course, I've heard a lot about my form," Simmons said. "It kept me on the bench for a while when I first joined Milwaukee. Harry Clarke, who was the manager, took one look at me and promptly decided I would never make a hitter. You couldn't blame him. He never had seen anyone with form like mine who could hit."

Simmons fell into a sad slump with the White Sox (must have been a contagious disease) and was ultimately benched. By 1936 he was playing for the Detroit Tigers. In the latter stages of his career with the Sox, as baseball was trying to emerge from the Depression, Simmons wrote a story offering advice to young ballplayers. He eagerly recommended baseball as a career.

"More young men should be playing baseball," Simmons wrote, "not only as a pastime, but if they have ambitions to become professional players. Baseball is overcoming the Depression, and there are going to be more chances for the young amateur or semipro player to land in the ranks of organized baseball."

Intriguingly, Simmons suggested just how the young baseball player could gain strength and ready himself for the rigors of the majors or minors. "Amateur and semipro players who wish to make baseball their profession should obtain the necessary rest and sleep," he said, as if talking to an elementary-school child. "Late hours, careless dieting, and dissipation have ruined many a young athlete. Consequently, in conclusion, my advice to the sandlotter is to get in shape carefully and remain in condition. That will be winning two-thirds of the battle if he has the natural physical and mental qualifications."

Junior Tried to Be Like Dad

Big Ed Walsh was an icon when he pitched, putting up such superb numbers that fans and fellow players marveled at his endurance. He prematurely burned out his arm and then surprised everyone by returning to baseball as an umpire in 1922, at the age of 41.

Only five years removed from being an active player, Walsh passed judgment on the on-field doings of some of his former teammates and opponents when he signed up to be an American League arbiter. In current times such a swift ascension likely would be regarded as a conflict of interest. Yet American League president Ban Johnson welcomed Walsh back.

"Baseball owes you such a position," Johnson told Walsh. "I think you are a man eminently qualified to fill one as an umpire."

Big Ed Walsh (right) and his son Ed Walsh Jr. pose together in the Sox dugout in 1930. Though both men played for the Sox at different times in their lives, Big Ed was undisputedly the better player.

Despite advancing to middle age, Walsh felt he was physically prepared to hold up during the hot July days of midseason.

"I have strength and health and ambition," Walsh said, "and it will be through no fault of mine if I do not justify Ban Johnson's confidence in me."

Walsh's American League umpiring days lasted exactly one season. If Walsh had lasted a bit longer, his situation might have become even more pressure-packed. His son, Ed Walsh Jr., joined the White Sox in 1928 and played parts of four seasons with the club, compiling a lifetime record of 11–24. He was not in the same league with his father as a thrower, but Dad was pretty proud to see his boy reach the big leagues.

Big Ed, who coached Notre Dame baseball after his big-league days ended with a coaching position with the Sox, sent Ed the younger to South Bend, Indiana for a pitching and classroom education.

"I want him to have a college education," the older pitcher said. "He's a good boy, and he's entitled to the best that I can give him, and that is why I am sending him to Notre Dame. He has the makings of a fine pitcher, I know that. I've taught him all I know, and he'll make good."

For one thing, Big Ed Walsh definitely expected his son to make more money than he did in his prime. As a White Sox rookie in 1904, Walsh's salary was $1,800 a year. When he won 40 games in 1908, a performance that would pay off with a salary of something like $25 million a century later, Walsh collected $3,500.

Sadly, Young Ed did not excel on the diamond. Nor did he enjoy a long and prosperous life. He was killed in a car crash in 1937 at the age of 32.

chapter 4

Stuck in the Second Division

Luke Appling takes batting practice before a game at Comiskey Park in 1940. He still holds many Sox records today, nearly 60 years after his retirement, and he was a bright spot on the second-division Sox of the 1940s.

City Series Pleasures

Somehow it figured that the White Sox, mired in a two-decade-long slump, played their best in games that didn't count in the standings. While the United States was stuck in World War II, the Sox continued to be distant also-rans during the 1940s.

Being a White Sox fan during this era was trying. The best the Sox could do was dominate the crosstown Chicago Cubs in the annual City Series. This was long before formal interleague play was sanctioned, so it was a rarity when the two Chicago teams met on the diamond. Each year the squads representing the Windy City's two major league clubs played a series to raise money for charity.

The series began in 1903, and it is hard to imagine now—with the clubs playing six times each summer in games that count—that fans actually cared enough about the exhibitions to be excited about bragging rights. Still playing lousy regularly scheduled baseball against the rest of the American League, the White Sox caught fire as the City Series calendar pages turned into the 1940s.

In 1940 the Sox won four out of the six games played. In 1941 the Sox swept the Cubs four games in a row. In 1942 the White Sox again won four of the six games. However, attendance was down, minds were focused on World War II, and the series was discontinued.

In the wake of the abandonment of the annual event, some intrepid White Sox fans printed up certificates claiming perpetual "superiority" over the Cubs. The message on the certificates read: "Whereas the South Side baseball club, hereinafter known as the White Sox, has once again demonstrated its superiority over the North Side baseball club, hereinafter unmentionable, this certificate entitles the bearer to WINDY CITY BRAGGING RIGHTS by virtue of being a lifelong White Sox fan (valid until Satan needs a space heater)."

Shortstops Need Not Apply

From 1930 to 1950 there was only one position where the White Sox were set, only one spot on the field that produced no worries for Chicago managers. Spunky shortstop Luke Appling owned the assignment. The future Hall of Famer was one of the White Sox's best players ever.

He was so reliable that nearly 60 years after his retirement, Appling still owns many team records. He played in the most White Sox games (2,422), came to bat the most times (8,856), and clouted the most hits (2,749). Appling batted .310 for his career and hit .388 in 1936 when he led the league in average. He won a second batting title in 1943 with a .328 average, and he nearly acquired a third when he hit .348 in 1940. Appling was a four-time All-Star.

Unfortunately for Appling, the White Sox fielded few other players of his caliber throughout the 1930s and 1940s. He was a lonely star, destined to never play on a pennant winner during his entire stay in Chicago. If you listened to Appling talk about his situation, however, it was not the state of the team he complained about. His nickname was Old Aches and Pains, and that's because Appling was always carping about a sickness, an injury, a wound, or another ailment. If Appling was taken seriously each time he moaned, he would have had an ambulance on permanent standby at Comiskey Park to whisk him to safety, and he would have had a constant intravenous blood transfusion pumping into his arm to keep him standing. The thing about Appling was that he talked a bad game, but he always came to play. Once in the lineup there was little evidence to suggest he was not at 100 percent.

Appling was born in High Point, North Carolina, in 1907 and was a sturdy 5'10" and 183 pounds. By comparison most of the exceptional shortstops of his day were gazelles, lighter on their feet and smaller in physical stature. Appling took many ground balls off his chest trying to play the funny hops, but he outhit his contemporaries who played the position. At his worst, there was no exaggerating Appling's woes in the field.

"He was pretty raw as a busher," White Sox mainstay pitcher Ted Lyons said. "But you could see he had big-league stuff in him. I never saw anybody better built to be a ballplayer. The first couple of years, though, it seemed as if he were the worst enemy I had on the field. In nearly every game I pitched, he would throw a couple of balls into the stands. Even his wife rode him for it. She said that it was a shame that he always had to ruin my ballgames."

White Sox fans got used to the fact that Appling was not going to be as graceful in the field as he was at bat. A certain number of errors were factored into expectations because of the way he roamed the hole. Appling understood that people did not consider him balletic with a glove. He once told a story to the old American League Service Bureau, an organization that wrote stories about players for public relations distribution.

Appling attended Oglethorpe University in Georgia for two years, where he learned he had the makings of a pro prospect. In the days before anyone dreamed up athletics scholarships, he was an undergraduate who worked one of the typical student jobs to earn his way through school. A waiter in a dormitory dining room as a freshman, Appling said he "never made an error. Never dropped a tray or broke a dish."

It was suggested that if Appling didn't bobble anything, then he surely must have mixed up an order or two. He denied it, though it sounded as if he had a twinkle in his eye as he spoke. "Not a chance," Appling said. "The other students took what I brought them or went without."

After his second season of college ball, Appling played in the minors in Atlanta, where he hit .326 in the Southern League. The White Sox spotted him and scooped him up. Through free swinging and diligent practice efforts in the field, Appling made himself popular in Chicago. Fans yelled, "Luuuke! Luuuke!" when his turn at bat arrived.

Appling was not a power hitter, but he drove pitchers mad with his persistence. He possessed the patience and the ability to foul off pitch after pitch to wear down throwers. Sometimes pitchers grew so frazzled trying to blow a fastball past Appling that they began yelling at him from the mound.

"When I saw a pitch I didn't like, I just fouled it off," Appling said. "It was easy." There are a thousand hitters who wish they could make such a claim. If it's so easy to get wood on any pitch, how come Nolan Ryan struck out more than 5,700 batters?

Appling enjoyed recalling the time he made Lefty Gomez dizzy during a game against the New York Yankees. "Gomez was pitching, and we were down by two runs," Appling said, describing one of the occupational hazards of competing against the Yankees at their best. "He threw me two balls right down the middle, and I didn't swing. Then I worked the count to three and two, and he came off the mound cussin' at me, saying I was going to start fouling them off and wearing him out. He called [catcher] Bill Dickey out to the mound for a conference. When Bill came back I asked him what was going on. Bill scratched his head and said he didn't know. The next thing you know, Gomez pitched out to me on three and two and put me on first. Joe McCarthy was the Yankees manager, and he was so mad he ran out to the mound before I even got close to first base. Lefty told him not to worry, that he'd get the next batter out. He did."

Sadly, that illustrated the White Sox's situation during Appling's years. He could make plays that would help them win, but more often he would be stranded on the base paths because assistance was in short supply.

For all his health worries, Appling's endurance was a plus. He did break a leg in 1938, and when he was inducted into the Army in 1943 at the height of World War II, he thought his ball playing days might be over. He was wrong. Instead of being shipped overseas to fight, Appling's assignment kept him in the United States as a hospital attendant. When he returned to the White Sox after the war, Appling could not only still make contact with a pitcher's best stuff, he played five more seasons.

Appling was one of the top hitting shortstops who played up until 1950. Reporters greatly enjoyed talking to the chatterbox, who might give them a story about how his body was falling apart or might wax eloquent about hitting talents. Sometimes he combined the two elements, leading sportswriters to believe he was on the verge of collapse, only to tout game-winning hits.

"He never tightens up," wrote *Chicago Tribune* baseball writer James Cruisenberry in 1950. "He doesn't know the meaning of stress and strain. When he goes up to bat, he doesn't strut, he ambles. Not even if the game depends on what he does up there does he show the slightest sign of anxiety. He walks or ambles up to the plate with a grin on his face. He has a grin for the opposing catcher and another one for the umpire, as if saying to them, 'Imagine sending me up here at a time like this, me with my aching back and sore feet. Why, I ought to be home in bed.'"

Ten minutes later, after working over the pitcher for a full count, and perhaps another six foul balls, Appling might swat a single to bring home the winning run.

Appling never really retired from baseball. After completing his playing days, he managed teams in the minor leagues; coached for the Detroit Tigers, Cleveland Indians, Kansas City Athletics, and Baltimore Orioles; and scouted for Kansas City before returning to coach for the White Sox at age 62. By then he had already been inducted into the Hall of Fame for his Sox field exploits.

"It's nice to be back home," Appling said.

Street Smarts, Not Book Learning

In 1947, some 28 years after the Black Sox Scandal tarnished the White Sox franchise and four years before Shoeless Joe Jackson died, eventual Pulitzer Prize–winning sports columnist Red Smith wrote a newspaper article based on a letter he received from a player who appeared in the majors only briefly. That player, Ben DeMott, had a locker next to Joe Jackson while with the Cleveland club, before Jackson was traded to the White Sox. DeMott, a pitcher, only spent parts of the 1910 and 1911 seasons with Cleveland, and his lifetime record was, alas, 0–4.

In his note to Smith, DeMott stuck up for Jackson, saying the young player he knew would never have taken a bribe to throw the World Series. Historians have concluded that there is little doubt Jackson was illiterate, though he worked hard to cover up this shortcoming. DeMott said he used to read Jackson's mail to him, but he never thought the player was a dummy.

"I submit that he was quite a guy in many ways," DeMott reported to Smith. "The greatest of all his gifts was a darned good and open mind. Joe was far from stupid. He merely lacked education. I have often wondered if an education would have taken much from his open-mindedness, as well as cluttered up his uncanny memory.

"As you may not know, he could point to any rule in the book and 'read' it to you, but with enough ad-libbed words to indicate he was reciting. He could do the same thing with the account of any game his wife had read to him. He may have changed much since we both left Cleveland; I wouldn't know. But the Joe Jackson I knew would never have taken a $5,000 bribe to throw a ballgame. He knew too well that discovery would prevent him from playing baseball."

Bargain Pickup

Baseball trades are analyzed with the same scrutiny as the government's foreign policy, and the twists and turns of the results are often remembered as long. One of the best trades the White Sox ever made brought the team southpaw Thornton Lee. It was a nothing deal at the time, merely marking a change of scenery for a few players who seemed imbedded in ruts.

In a three-team arrangement, the Cleveland Indians obtained Jack Salveson, the Washington Senators obtained pitcher Earl Whitehill, and the White Sox cleaned their clocks by obtaining Thornton Lee. Salveson finished 9–9 lifetime. Whitehill was at the end of a 17-year career, and finished under .500 during his last three seasons with the Indians and Cubs. Lee, however, who had struggled through a rough three seasons with Cleveland, blossomed. He won 12 or more games six times between 1937 and 1947 for the White Sox, including posting a 22-win season in 1941. Not even the most optimistic White Sox official could have imagined such a wonderful payback for the trade.

"It was the best break I ever got," Lee said of the trade during his terrific 1941 run. "If I had stayed with the Tribe, I'd probably still be waiting for a chance to start regularly. The Indians always got away to a fast start and worked four or five pitchers in turn. The rest of us just cooled our heels on the bench."

Lee credited Sox manager Jimmie Dykes and coach Muddy Ruel for making him a better pitcher. But he also said that giving up smoking was a good idea, too. He had been throwing at 190 pounds. When he bagged the smokes, he went on an eating binge and brought his weight up to 220 pounds. The heft gave his fastball more velocity, Lee said.

"I couldn't keep my head out of the icebox," he said.

Dykes's Tight Ship

No one not named Comiskey had more invested in trying to make the White Sox into a winner than Jimmie Dykes, who managed the Pale Hose from 1934 to 1946 for 1,850 games, the most in team history. He also probably accumulated the most frustration in team history, despite being a savvy baseball man with an innate sense of humor that likely kept him sane as he tried to revive the fortunes of the Black Sox Scandal–marred club.

Dykes was a stellar player for Connie Mack's Philadelphia Athletics, an All-Star second and third baseman who broke in during the 1918 season and played 2,282 games with a lifetime .280 average. He greatly admired Mack, and he considered him a mentor worth following as a manager.

When Dykes was about to become Sox manager, he turned to Mack for words of wisdom. "Be yourself, Jimmie," Mack said. "Don't let your new job get you down, although there will be times when you will wish someone else was manager. Get to know your players and their limitations. Play a hunch now and then, and do not become discouraged if some of them go wrong. No manager can guess right on every occasion."

During Dykes's days, the White Sox set up spring training in Pasadena, California. He called the two-week train trip back to Chicago to start the regular season "The Blue Shirt Express." The team stopped by day to play an exhibition game, then hopped back on the train for overnight travel.

"We slept on the train, never saw the inside of a hotel," Dykes said in his autobiography, *You Can't Steal First Base*, coauthored with Charles Dexter. "The same three Pullman porters clamored for ballclub assignments each spring. We had three Pullmans and a club car, and we talked baseball from morning to midnight."

Dykes said the train parked on a side track, and the players were given itineraries telling them where they could stop to eat and obtain baths. "We slept late, dressed, and went into town for breakfast, then took a cab to the ballpark. It was life alfresco and an important part of our baseball education."

Players of the modern era would riot before living such a lifestyle.

Dykes was a fun-loving guy who knew all of the angles from his playing days. It was a challenge for a White Sox player who wanted to stay out late to put one over on the manager. Dykes had done it all and seen it all. During a road trip to New York, rainouts kept the team imprisoned in its hotel. Dykes figured the troops might be getting antsy and some might defy his midnight curfew. So he planted his butt in a seat in the lobby and staked out the scene. Sure enough, three players missed the deadline. Two showed up at 2:30 AM, eyes wide when they spotted Dykes. Dykes tolerated not a word of dissent and immediately informed them they would be fined $500 each. The third unaccounted-for player did not even show before Dykes went to sleep.

The next day Dykes approached him and asked what time he went to bed. The player said he was in bed by midnight. Dykes roared not to lie to him and fined him $500, too. All three of the violators were married men.

The next season Dykes realized his team was densely populated with night owls who seemed to get more out of their evening jaunts than they did performing at the park during the day. Four players seemed to be regular rulebreakers. Early in the new season, thinking back to the errant threesome of the year before, Dykes dreamed up a strategy he hoped would halt any misguided late-night carousing.

Dykes called a team meeting. He had written a letter that he said was going to be tacked up on a bulletin board and mailed to players' wives, and then he read it aloud to the players. "Dear Madam," Dykes wrote. "Will you kindly let me know where your husband goes after midnight on the road? Thus far I've been unable to find out who he spends his time with. I don't want to have him trailed. I don't want to fine him, as I know you need the money. If you get this information, please rush it to me. Jimmie Dykes." Then Dykes asked his players if they had any questions. Uh, no.

After the meeting one infielder, however, approached Dykes and said to fine him all he wanted, but to please never send such a letter to his wife. The White Sox got the message, and Dykes didn't have much misbehavior to worry about that season.

When World War II ended, and all of the servicemen ballplayers returned to their teams to jump-start peacetime baseball once more, Dykes once noticed star hurler Ted Lyons joking with Red Sox star Ted Williams before an at-bat. Lyons had always been a very serious moundsman, so Dykes was curious about what was going on. After the at-bat, Dykes asked his pitcher what was up. Lyons relayed this conversation:

"Where would you like me to put the ball, lieutenant?" Lyons said he asked Williams.

"Is this an official request, captain?" Williams responded.

"It certainly is."

Williams held his bat out over the plate about waist high and said, "Right here."

"Very well, sir."

Surprisingly, after the little charade, Lyons actually threw the pitch to the spot Williams requested. However, Williams was laughing so hard he couldn't even swing.

Dykes was known as the Earl Weaver of his time, a manager who could debate and bait umpires with the best of them. He made them laugh, and he made them cry, though he rarely changed their minds. Umpires knew that if there was a questionable play, Dykes would rush from the dugout and give them heck for a little while. Once, making fun of his own image, Dykes wrote a magazine story about how some of his best friends were umpires and when he dashed onto the field he was not doing so to criticize them, but to generously offer them help and advice.

Charles Comiskey had given way to son Louis Comiskey, who died young in 1938 and yielded ownership of the team to Mrs. Grace Comiskey, Louis's widow. During a typical Dykes argument with umpire Jack Quinn, Dykes said he felt hot breath on his neck and Quinn bellowed, "Who the heck is this?"

To Dykes's amazement, standing next to him was 15-year-old Charles Comiskey, Grace's son, wearing a White Sox uniform and seeking to get his licks in on the argument. "Meet Mr. Charles Comiskey, Mr. Quinn," Dykes said, graciously playing intermediary. "Mr. Comiskey is going to own the Sox one day."

"I don't care if he owns the Tribune Tower right now," Dykes attributed to Quinn. "Get him off the field!"

Dykes was an all-around dude, an accomplished bowler and golfer, as well as a prolific and accomplished raconteur. During the 1930s Dykes committed to playing in a Philadelphia Knights of Columbus golf tournament when the Sox returned to the City of Brotherly Love. The Sox and the A's had a doubleheader that day, however, and one game went into 11 innings. Dykes was in a bind. As soon as the games ended, he dashed to the course, not arriving until 7:40 PM. Daylight was on the wane, but Dykes played 18 holes in 65 minutes (sunset was five minutes away), shooting an 86 and helping his team win the first-place trophy. As long as he was there, Dykes decided to stick around for the ensuing dinner dance.

After managing for some years, Dykes was asked what rules of thumb he followed in surviving the stressful job. He listed several basic tenets players should abide by. Then he said, "A manager should own a sense of humor. If he does not, some of the play of his men may turn his hair gray, or get him to talking to himself."

With many second-division finishes, Dykes knew what he was talking about when it came to gray hair. But he did follow his own advice to maintain a sense of humor. Before the 1938 season, the wife of a dinner host at a California outing where some relaxed imbibing took place cajoled Dykes to have his fortune told—and then informed him how rotten the season would be.

"I hate to tell you this," she said. "It's bad. It's tough. I see a bad first half for your team. Many injuries. Serious ones."

Within a short period of time the White Sox suffered injuries to four players. Overall, the team finished 65–83, in sixth place that season—mirroring many Sox finishes throughout the 1930s and 1940s.

When things were at their bleakest, and every sad prediction was coming true, Dykes sent a telegram to the fortune teller saying, "Serve milk next time I'm over."

There were no published reports about any Dykes return visit or of him sitting for additional prognostication.

chapter 5

1950s Rejuvenation at Last

Jim Rivera, who led the American League in triples in 1953, typified the 1950s White Sox.

The Go-Go White Sox

Starting in 1951 with the arrival of Orestes "Minnie" Minoso, a terror on the basepaths, the theme, the style...heck, the *music* of the Chicago White Sox began to change. Concurrently, the Sox buried the image of the forlorn days of the 1920s, 1930s, and 1940s that followed the Black Sox Scandal curse.

"Let's go, go, go, White Sox, we're with you all the way. You're always going out there to do your best. We're glad to have you out here in the Middle West." How many baseball teams had theme music that fans could sing along with besides "Take Me Out to the Ballgame"? "Let's Go Go Go White Sox" was not only a catchy tune, it was a catchy way of life. Suddenly, the White Sox were a running team with base stealers galore.

Swift outfielder Jim Busby was an ever-present danger on the basepaths. Shortstop Luis Aparicio appeared and led the American League in steals nine years in a row. Minoso was a wild man on the bases, intimidating outfielders into bad throws and repeated misjudgments. Baseball was still pretty much in love with the long ball, stemming from the Babe-Ruth-Yankees era of the 1920s, but the White Sox, under new manager Paul Richards, developed their own brand of ball that harkened back to the strategic one-run-at-a-time days of the dead-ball era.

The White Sox had been living in the dark ages since Chick Gandil and Swede Risberg hatched their nefarious World-Series-fix plot, with losing season piled upon losing season as if they were just fresh bales of hay. The 1950s offered a new beginning. Not only did the White Sox acquire fresh stars, they played a fresh, exciting style of baseball. Spectators at Comiskey Park watched players who actually seemed to have fun playing. The team also believed it could win. Such an attitude had been missing for many years. Not even Jimmie Dykes could talk all of his guys into becoming believers.

Jim Rivera grew up in New York and broke into the majors in 1952. He was another Sox player who would have been at home lining up in spikes for the start of the national AAU 100-yard dash, another player who typified the Sox of the time.

Rivera led the American League in triples in 1953, smacking 16 of the leg-it-out hits. It takes wheels to get around the bases fast enough to produce so many triples in a season. And that's when all of the ballparks contained God's green grass, making the ball roll slower than it did later when stadiums introduced artificial turf.

"If it was Astroturf," Rivera said much later, "boy, I would have had more. On Astroturf, you know they shoot out like a bullet."

Slugging often makes up for a passel of shortcomings, but when a team's game is predicated on speed, it helps to do the little things well. Pitching always counts, but fielding counts more than it might with a team of bombers in the lineup. The White Sox had strength down the middle, with superb fielding at shortstop, second base, and center field.

Luke Appling wound up his days as the sole proprietor of White Sox shortstopping in 1950. He was succeeded by Venezuelan flash Chico Carrasquel, and Luis Aparicio came along in 1956, another future Hall of Famer, who led the league in fielding eight consecutive years.

Like Carrasquel, Aparicio was from Venezuela—and he still lives there. They established the mold of spunky Latin American infielders, making them heroes in the region and setting the stage as role models for new generations of big leaguers. Aparicio's English was limited, but he got along well with his teammates, especially keystone partner Fox.

Carrasquel was a four-time All-Star—bridging the gap between Appling and Aparicio—and the grandfather of the legacy of major league Venezuelan shortstops. It was Carrasquel who brought Aparicio to the attention of White Sox management. Afterward, another Venezuelan youngster grew up idolizing Aparicio and dreaming of the day he, too, would become a White Sox shortstop. That's how it turned out for Ozzie Guillen, now the White Sox manager.

"I took Looie from there to here," Carrasquel said many years later. He was a shortstop in the Venezuelan League. His father was one of the greatest shortstops who ever played in Venezuela. Ozzie is carrying out a great tradition. Because of me, Aparicio, and Davey Conception (a former Reds star), all the kids in Venezuela want to play shortstop."

During his playing days, Aparicio was invariably referred to as Little Looie in newspapers, just as second baseman Nellie Fox was called Little Nel. It must have been a rule that average-sized humans in sports had to be described as little, or that players were considered small if they did not tower over the sportswriters.

Aparicio was an instant wonder with the White Sox. Once Carrasquel dropped him off at Sox spring training, Chico signed his own ticket out of town. Aparicio was so good, so fast, that the White Sox traded away their All-Star and gave the starting job to the newcomer for the 1956 season.

"I came from a baseball-playing family," Aparicio said. "My father used to be a ballplayer. My uncle also used to be a ballplayer. They took me to the ballpark often, and each helped me a lot. I think you need three things to be a good shortstop: good hands, quick reflexes, and smarts. And I think I had them all, so I guess I turned out to be a good shortstop."

Aparicio gave credit to Carrasquel for his influence. "Chico was my idol," Aparicio said. "He's a tremendous guy, and he helped me a lot."

Just as Carrasquel tutored Aparicio, Aparicio advised Guillen, who came to Chicago at age 21.

"I've never seen [Aparicio] play," Guillen said, "but he told me a lot about Chicago. I'm not going to try to play like him. I just want to keep my job and help the team win. If people say I'm a super shortstop and we lose, it doesn't mean anything."

Guillen spent 16 years in the majors, leading the American League in fielding as a rookie in 1985 before becoming a coach and manager. As field boss he led the 2005 White Sox to their first World Series title since 1917.

In the summer of 2006, to commemorate their slick and dominating infield play, the White Sox unveiled a special bronze double-statue of Aparicio and Nellie Fox turning a double play. Aparicio was emotional and tearful, that day. One reason was the absence of Fox, who had long before died of cancer.

Jacob Nelson Fox was a genial man, but he always had a pug-
nacious look on his face because he chewed tobacco. Fox's
cheek bulged larger than the baseball he sought to field, it
seemed. That was his trademark as much as his slap hitting, spray-
ing singles all over the infield, or scooping up grounders.

Fox was even slighter than Aparicio. He was going to do better
with guile than force, and his clever fielding carried him into the
Hall of Fame. Fox was not ashamed to choke up on the bat, and
he realized the value of the hit-and-run and putting runners into
scoring position, and he was more willing to sacrifice for the
common good than most.

Sportswriters often said Fox was a throwback player, the kind
of guy who didn't mind getting dirty around second base when the
dust flew. He was seen as the type of player who would have
thrived in 1915 as well as 1955. To prove the point, out of the blue
came a letter from Ty Cobb, then still the sport's all-time hits king.
Extolling Fox's skills, Cobb praised the Sox second-sacker as a
player who would have excelled back when the game was played
differently. Especially among those who knew Cobb, it was understood that this was a compliment of the highest order from the
man many considered the best ever to play the game.

Fox played his prime years for Al Lopez, one of the most
esteemed managers of the period and one of the most admired
White Sox managers in their history. Fox was an All-Star for the
Sox every year but one between 1951 and 1963. That is no fluke.
A selection record like that deserves respect.

"You have to say that Nellie is the hustlingest player in the
league," Lopez said.

When a manager says something like that about you, it's clear
you are one of his favorites. Fox had a great passion for the game,
and even when managers told him to take a rest, to take a break of
some kind, he resisted. As the end of the 1951 season approached,
Fox suffered an injured thumb. A small injury for the man in the street,
but a potentially devastating one for a hitter. Fox hit .247 the year
before and was making himself into the ballplayer he would eventually become by hitting over .300. Even manager Paul Richards,

however, underestimated Fox's pride when the boss offered to sit Fox out to preserve the average.

"Nothing doing," Fox said. "I don't want to rest."

"What?" Richards queried. "Don't you want to hit .300?"

"Yeah, I want to hit .300, but playing, not sitting on the bench," Fox said.

Even with the injury, Fox actually raised his average to .313 by the end of the season.

During the 1957 season, Richards, who had moved on to managing the Baltimore Orioles, still couldn't say enough good things about Fox.

"Of all the stars now in the game, he's the greatest example to young players, and even to players yet unborn," Richards said. "In fact, he's *baseball* to all of young America."

There is a theory that slenderly built players are not built for the long haul or the long schedule. These players need to save themselves, it is suggested. When the brutally hot days of July and August take a toll, it is presumed they will wilt. Thinking ahead, sometimes Richards ordered Fox to the clubhouse to get out of the sun during spring training. Why waste energy then? Then Richards caught Fox sneaking back into the dugout in disguise, just so he could watch.

One time Fox stooped to field a ground ball, only to see it take a bad bounce off a pebble or something, and smack him in the face. The runner was safe. Fox made no comment, and the game continued until Carrasquel called time and jogged into the dugout to inform the rest of the team that Fox was badly hurt. The trainer accompanied Carrasquel back to the field and examined Fox, who had one tooth knocked out and others loosened, as well as a cut lip.

"It's nothing," Fox said. "I'll stay in."

Some baseball players are earmarked for greatness in the cradle. Their success is preordained the moment they take their first step or juggle their first ball as toddlers. Their hand-eye coordination, their speed, and their talent are evident even to a passerby who wears glasses so thick they would blur newsprint at four inches. Fox was not one of the naturals. Even Richards, his biggest fan, didn't think much of Little Nell's major league prospects when they first met in spring training of 1951. Richards said Fox couldn't field or hit and made the double-play pivot cross-legged. But he responded enthusiastically to coaching and soaked up every lesson and tip.

"He was so eager to learn and improve himself that he wore everybody out," Richards said. "He was the first one on the field and the last to leave. But it paid off."

Fox married his childhood sweetheart, Joanne Statler, who was a year behind him in junior high school. She said Fox never aspired to be anything but a ballplayer and displayed so much devotion to the sport and so little interest in school that Fox's mother wrote to Connie Mack, then the pooh-bah of the Philadelphia Athletics, asking him to sign Fox. Remarkably, the men clicked, and Fox was off to a minor league club and ultimately Mack's team.

Fox's wife said that during his first years in the minors, starting in 1944, she rode with Nellie's parents to games in Lancaster, Pennsylvania, and Hagerstown, Maryland.

"I didn't like baseball, but I must've liked him," she said.

Roger Kahn, the famous baseball writer who has followed the sport for more than half a century, once decided to give Fox his due as a singular singles-hitter rather than focusing on another power-hitter story. His first step was tracking Fox down in his rural Pennsylvania home of St. Thomas, a tiny burg of about 1,000, where residents were at least as partial to deer hunting as baseball.

Kahn called information and had an entertaining conversation with the operator.

"Where is St. Thomas?" she said.

"It's in Pennsylvania," replied Kahn.

"Never heard of it," she said.

"Nellie Fox lives there," Kahn said.

"Who's Nellie Fox?" she asked.

"He's the best singles-hitter in baseball," Kahn said.

"Can't he hit home runs?" the operator asked.

In a way, they were both right. Fox hit only 35 home runs in his 19-year major league career. But his lifetime average was .288, and he was finally invited into the Hall of Fame in 1997.

Fox opened a 20-lane bowling alley near Chambersburg, Pennsylvania, in 1956 and expected that would be the main focus of his business life once he ceased playing baseball. Fox retired in 1965, but he didn't get as much time to enjoy bowling as he hoped. Sadly, he died of cancer in 1975.

Forever Is a Long Time

In the winter of 1956, a few months before the baseball season began, George "Buck" Weaver, the old Black Sox Scandal figure, collapsed and died of a heart attack while walking along the sidewalk in Chicago. He was 65 years old and went to his grave proclaiming his innocence in the 1919 World Series fix.

Historians who labored so hard to sort through the clues, the hearsay, and the evidence generally agreed that Weaver was the most innocent of the parties banned from baseball for life for partaking in the sordid incident. Weaver said he never gave less than 100 percent in the games against the Cincinnati Reds, and that his only crime was failure to report a bribe offer in connection with the scheme. He neither participated nor knew what was happening when the fix went down, he said many times.

Weaver joined the White Sox in 1912, shortly before his 22nd birthday. He was a wizard with a glove and batted .272 in his nine major league seasons. The longer he played, the better Weaver got. He hit .333 in the 1917 World Series victory over the New York Giants and hit .324 in the 1919 World Series, where his actions were looked upon as suspicious. In 27 fielding chances during that Series, Weaver performed flawlessly.

From the period at the end of the 1920 season through the trial that acquitted the players of complicity in any fix, Weaver always professed innocence. He sought to sever his case from

Buck Weaver, shown here catching a ball in 1916, professed his innocence in the Black Sox Scandal until he died.

the others in the courtroom, and in 1922, soon after his banishment by commissioner Kenesaw Mountain Landis, Weaver first petitioned for reinstatement. He was turned down. Throughout the years he tried several more times, always spoke up in his own defense, and rallied friends, family, and other supporters to take up his cause. During one of his attempts to sway the commissioner, Weaver turned in a petition with 30,000 names asking that he be exonerated.

Nothing dented the stone wall Landis threw up, and even after Landis died in 1944, no commissioner offered the hope of clemency. In 1953 Weaver wrote to Ford Frick, the last time he directly appealed to a commissioner seeking reinstatement. In his letter, Weaver said, "then I was suspended for doing something wrong, which I knew nothing about."

Gradually, Weaver aged beyond the ability to resume playing baseball, and any reinstatement would have been more symbolic than it would have provided any tangible benefit. He went on to a career as a pari-mutuel racetrack clerk. Yet the campaign to clear Weaver's name did not die with him. For decades thereafter, small numbers of surviving relatives led drives to obtain reinstatement.

In 2003, to draw attention to Weaver's situation, Weaver supporters conducted a Chicago rally during All-Star week leading up to baseball's midsummer showcase game at Comiskey Park. One of Weaver's nieces, Patricia Scanlon Anderson, then 77, said she and her late sister were raised by their uncle. "I fight because I owe him," she said.

Another niece, Marjorie Follett, then 89, spent more than 30 years working on Weaver's behalf. "For heaven's sake, Buck is an innocent man," she said. "And I just want to clear his name." Follett appealed to commissioner Bud Selig with the proposition, "Wouldn't you rather be known as the man who cleared Buck Weaver?"

Selig has not shown any indication that he would.

"Buck Weaver was banned from baseball for life," Follett said. "Even though he's no longer here, he has served his sentence, and he served it as an innocent man."

When Weaver died in January 1956 he was praised as the best fielding third baseman of his time and in some quarters was portrayed as a wronged man. Some White Sox players still living, who were on the team during the Black Sox Scandal and were lumped together as Clean Sox, stood up for Weaver.

Ray Schalk, the Hall of Fame catcher who was suspicions something was amiss, but who was so unaware of the scheme that he accused at least one pitcher of not trying and challenged him to a fight, called Weaver "the greatest third baseman I ever saw." Schalk said, "I used to run into him at the racetrack and generally gave him a cigar. Last time I saw him was about a year ago, out at my bowling alley. I introduced him to a lot of the fellows, and we had a pretty good time."

Urban "Red" Faber, the Hall of Fame pitcher, also remembered Weaver fondly.

"I played baseball with Weaver, and I played cards with him," Faber said, "and I found him as honest as could be. No one can ever be certain about 1919, I guess. Weaver was a wonderful competitor, a fellow who played baseball because he loved it."

Weaver, Faber said, never wanted to leave the field when a game or practice ended. Weaver said being kicked out of baseball was a physical hurt that he never recovered from.

El Señor

It is telling that all of the *Sporting News* coverage of Al Lopez's managerial career with the White Sox between 1957 and 1965 casually refers to him in headlines as El Señor. That was a commentary on how few Latin American baseball stars populated the sport at the time and especially how few Latinos were in positions of authority.

Later in life, as the man who brought the Sox their only other pennant between 1919 and 2005 relaxed in retirement in his hometown of Tampa, Florida, he became known as Señor Al as a gesture of respect. An admired catcher as a player, Lopez realized greater fame later in life as a manager. During a 12-year period from 1948 to 1960, when the New York Yankees dominated baseball, only two American League clubs were able to outfox them and steal a pennant. The Cleveland Indians of 1954 represented the American League in the World Series, and the White Sox of 1959 did likewise. Both teams were managed by Al Lopez.

Lopez always retained his Tampa ties. When he broke into the majors in 1928, he became the first native of the city on Florida's west coast to make the big leagues. Lopez played just three games with Brooklyn that season but remained in the majors for 19 seasons, catching 1,918 games behind the plate. He was known for his astuteness in calling a game and his handling of pitchers, and in 1977 he was inducted into the Baseball Hall of Fame. So revered is he in his home community, Lopez is the namesake of a baseball stadium used in spring training.

Al Lopez (right) shares a laugh with Yankees manager Casey Stengel prior to a series of games in 1957. In 1959 Lopez brought the White Sox their only pennant between 1919 and 2005.

When Lopez assumed command of the White Sox for the 1957 season, it was the first genuine sustained period of optimism the franchise had known since Charles A. Comiskey and manager Kid Gleason ran the club. Fresh off his successful stint in Cleveland, Lopez did not fear the Yankees dynasty; he wanted to challenge it and overcome it. If there was intimidation coursing through the blood of American League players who year after year watched Mickey Mantle, Yogi Berra, and Whitey Ford hog all of the team glory, Lopez wanted a transfusion that would affect bloodstreams and attitudes. So in spring training Lopez predicted the Sox would win the pennant. Such daring talk had been little-heard on the South Side of Chicago for many years. Nostradomus, Lopez was not. The Sox did not claim the title. But they gave the Yanks a serious run, finishing second with 90 wins. An upbeat era in White Sox baseball was underway.

The White Sox stayed in the pennant race mathematically until the last week of the season with a group of hotshot players still popular among Sox aficionados—Billy Pierce, Minnie Minoso, Sherm Lollar, Nellie Fox, and Luis Aparicio, among others.

Astutely reviewing the big picture, Lopez said the Sox would have surpassed the Yankees if they had better relief pitching.

"If we had a stopper, we could have won it easily," Lopez said. "The games we lost in the late innings were criminal. We dropped nine games in the ninth and seven in the eighth. In extra innings, we won eight and lost 10."

Lopez was not a yeller as a field leader. He managed with restraint, but with firmness. No man is popular with 100 percent of the populace, the players he handles, or opponents, but Lopez, who by the time he was managing wore trademark wire-rimmed glasses, made many more friends than enemies with his demeanor.

"Al could best be described as low pressure," *Chicago Tribune* sportswriter Edward Prell penned. "Everything he does is without ostentation. It's a rarity that in baseball, which produces intense rivalries that sometimes spill over into personal feuds, you never hear a harsh word directed at the Señor. He's a nice guy without working at it."

Lopez never ripped players in public. He always insisted on closed-door office meetings to criticize, and players appreciated that.

"He knew which guy to pat on the back and which guy to chew out," said outfielder Jim Landis. "One thing about him, when he chewed somebody out, it was in his office. That to me is the right way to do that, definitely. I don't think he was strict. He was a good guy to play for.

"Our record, the way we played, it was something for someone to hit 20 home runs in a season. Skipper used to say that we had three leadoff hitters in Luis, Nellie, and me, and that was our biggest asset. We were going to get some guys on base."

Born Alfonso Ramon Lopez in Tampa in 1908, the 5'11", 165-pound Lopez was described as "the only full-blooded Spaniard in the big leagues." Lopez was such a good fielder that in 1941, when he backstopped the Pirates for 114 games, he never allowed a passed ball all season.

Much later, Tino Martinez, another Tampa native who had success in the big leagues, said of Lopez, "His name will live forever."

Lopez inherited the Go-Go Sox routine established by Paul Richards and nurtured by Marty Marion, and in evaluating his personnel he saw that major changes were unlikely and that he had to win with the hand dealt him. In a time before free agency there was no quick fix to add home-run hitters to the lineup simply by signing a check. Chicago's hopes were built around the small-ball game.

"At Chicago, we had no long-ball hitting," Lopez said. "Just guys that could run and field. We won our share of games running."

Lopez was greatly admired as an evenhanded manager whose teams would always be in contention, but the Yankees drove him crazy. He set records by overseeing clubs that during his first nine years as field boss never finished below second place. The problem was that they almost always finished *in* second place, one spot behind the Yankees. It was two pennants in nine tries for Lopez, and after feeling he had the club to overtake the Yanks in 1957, only to falter in the last week, he burned to disrupt the New York dynasty. In the middle of that season the White Sox lost a one-run game to the Yanks in 11 innings, and when it was over Lopez smashed his hand down on his desk and growled, "Just one game I'd like to win for these people!"

Lopez was one of those devoted baseball men who said he loved the sport so much he would have played for free. Future Players Union executive director Marvin Miller would have clutched his chest if he ever heard any of his members say such a thing. When Lopez was playing, even many of the stars played for the next closest thing to free, although he did make a $16,500 salary one season.

After Lopez guided the White Sox to the 1959 pennant, owner Bill Veeck rewarded his manager with a $60,000 contract. At the press conference to announce the deal, Veeck showed off a blown-up 6'x10' replica of a contract featuring Lopez's name with the salary figure to be filled in.

"He is certainly making more than the president of the corporation," Veeck said.

Lopez once got a chuckle out of hearing that he was "anti-Yankee," as if the rest of the American League was not.

"I'm *anti* any club that wins all of the time, and I hope that some day people will hate the White Sox for winning all of the time," he said.

That has yet to occur. However, in 1959, much as if he had risked a glimpse into a crystal ball and uttered a straightforward pronouncement, though proven incorrect before, Lopez took the same hazardous guess again. The Yankees, he said before that season, appeared ripe to be taken.

The Third Fielder Up the Middle

The way baseball teams line up, there are only two middle infielders—a shortstop and a second baseman. They are incredibly important fielders to the health and future of the team in the standings and to any pitcher. Similarly, the man who holds down center field is a critical piece on the chess board. The center fielder usually is as fleet as an antelope and has carte blanche to roam right and to roam left to pick off the fly balls he feels are within his reach and perhaps out of the reach of the left- and right-fielders.

The complementary piece to Luis Aparicio and Nellie Fox during the Go-Go 1950s was fleet-footed outfielder Jim Landis. Landis broke in with the White Sox for the 1957 season and spent most of his 11-year major league career with Chicago. He could field with the aplomb of Willie Mays. But Landis at first could not outhit his own mother. This placed manager Al Lopez in a tricky position.

Lopez knew the Sox needed Landis's glove. He was so fine that he prompted comparisons to Tris Speaker, and some felt he had the range of buffalo on the plains. But how many automatic outs could a team that was hoping for a pennant afford? The White Sox could not hide many weak bats, and before the advent of the designated hitter, there was always going to be a write-off in the order with the day's pitcher.

Things reached critical mass one day when Landis struck out five times in a game. The situation looked grim for the youngster. Was he headed back to the minors? Was he going to have his rear-end planted on the bench and glued to it?

Lopez surprised everyone from Landis to his teammates and the sportswriters by making no change at all. He felt the 23-year-old player's shortcomings could be overcome that season, and that he would improve in the future.

"What could I have gained by benching Landis?" Lopez asked. "I could have broken the boy's confidence."

Landis hit only .212 as a rookie, but he hit in the .270s each of the next two seasons. Lopez was patient enough to wait out Landis's adjustment period. Most often the contributions of a player are more evenly balanced, but Landis's fielding gifts far outweighed his contributions with the bat, they were that extraordinary.

"It may sound a little cocky, but you had to feel this way," Landis said. "There was no ball I couldn't catch. That to me was real determination, and if you haven't got that, you're not a good outfielder."

Landis proved his bravado was accurate when he won Gold Glove awards in 1960, 1961, 1962, 1963, and 1964. He also made the American League All-Star team in 1962.

Throughout the late 1950s and beyond, Landis had a bird's-eye view of the magic Aparicio and Fox performed in the infield. He was standing only about 100 feet behind them when they dove and made stops on hot grounders or leapt and plucked scorching line drives out of the air.

"They were outstanding, you know," Landis said. "Every once in a while Luis would make a play, and maybe I should have been moving to back him up in case he didn't make the play, but I'd stand there in awe and go, 'God, he made that play.' He made every play in the book, as far as I'm concerned. Left, right, in whatever way, he made it. When he went in the hole, what an arm. He had a terrific arm. And look at Nellie's fielding averages. That will tell you how good a fielder he was. They were both tremendous, and they're in the Hall of Fame. That proves a big point."

chapter 6

The Hard-Throwing Lefty from Detroit

Sox manager Al Lopez (left), the man who led the Sox to the 1959 pennant, talks with pitcher Billy Pierce.

Growing Up with the White Sox

Billy Pierce was still an unfinished canvas when he was traded from his hometown Detroit Tigers to the White Sox, the team that became his hometown team. He was still only 22 but felt that if given a regular turn in a pitching rotation, he could show he belonged in the big leagues.

The White Sox were coming off of nearly 30 seasons of false hopes and dashed expectations. They were open to suggestions. Pierce may have gotten his big chance a year too early, when he was still learning his trade, since he finished 7–15 with the Sox in 1949 before he blossomed into a steady winner.

But from a downtrodden team with its face rubbed into the dirt by the best of the American League each season, the White Sox also seemed to be blossoming. The kids that wildman general manager Frank Lane traded for showed they had the makings of something. Lane was an experimental chef, tossing a pinch of that and half glass of this into the mixture, desperately seeking the proper ingredients for a tasty dish that would make people happy.

"In 1949 and 1950, we were just a team changing," Pierce said. "Frank Lane was changing players all of the time. But I came to Chicago in 1949. Nellie came in 1950. Minnie Minoso came along in 1951, along with Jim Rivera and a few others. All of a sudden, we were a team that had a little bit of excitement going. Teams knew that if they were playing us now they were playing a decent ballclub. Before, we were just another team. I hate to knock any team, but the St. Louis Browns and Philadelphia A's never had great teams in those years. And Washington had problems."

In 1951 the White Sox finished 81–73 and finished fourth in the American League. They weren't contenders going head-to-head with the Yankees, Red Sox, and Indians, but they were no longer pushovers.

"There were a lot of good battles going on," Pierce said. "Cleveland had great hitting. The Yankees had hitting and pitching, and that's why they won. I didn't like the Yankees, for sure. They were tough."

There were no giddy predictions being voiced in spring training that the White Sox were going to overtake the Yankees, but as each season passed, the lineup became a bit better and the pitching became a little bit stronger. The Sox finished 81–73 again in 1952 and 89–65 in 1953. No more patsies. Three winning seasons in a row, the latter being 24 games over .500, called for respect.

During the 1950s, Pierce was one of the soundest southpaws in baseball. Even though he was selected for six American League All-Star teams during the decade, he still pitched somewhat in the shadow of that "other lefty," Whitey Ford. Ford shined during the regular season, as did Pierce, but more importantly for his reputation, Ford starred in the World Series each October, on a national stage. Ford was a clutch pitcher and a deserving Hall of Famer with a lifetime winning percentage of .690. No one dared suggest he didn't belong with the greats. Yet Pierce and Ford had a sharp rivalry going. The difference, most of the time, was that Ford had the better support. All things were not equal. Pierce had to be a little bit better because Ford always had more punch in the lineup.

"People would always ask me, 'Is it tough pitching against Ford?'" Pierce joked. "I'd say, 'No, no, no.' It was the other eight Yankees that got me. I'd get Whitey out alright, but the Yankees didn't make mistakes. They did not beat themselves. They didn't make errors. They threw to the right bases, and they were just a good, solid ballclub always.

"People say, 'Oh, the great hitting of the Yankees and this and that.' Check out some of their World Series games, and you'll see some 2–1, 1–0, and 3–2 games they had on the winning side. If you look through the box score, you'll see no errors. It helps."

Managers got gray hair, hitters bashed water coolers, and pitchers heaved their gloves when they ran into the Yankee buzz saw and usually came away disappointed. The Yankees either started fast and put away the whole field by the first turn, or they lurked and made a run, giving the other leading teams a crick in the neck looking back at them charging. During the 1950s the Yankees drove the rest of the American League nuts with their superiority.

"Oh, there definitely was frustration," Pierce said. "You may have a good team and you'd play a good series. We'd win two out of three or something like that. But then we'd go off and play somebody else, and our team that may not have had the experience of the Yankees, we'd be so elated from winning that I don't think the drive was quite there. At the same time, the Yankees were going on to Kansas City, and they'd win three quick games. You wouldn't, and what you gained, you lost.

"You could never get rid of them. That was the problem. They were always right at the top."

Steady Improvement

If the Yankees had a hex on the White Sox and the rest of the American League, the Sox slowly came to believe in themselves, to believe that they fielded a better team and that the league pennant did not belong to New York out of divine right. As the Go-Go Sox players matured and came together, they began to ask, "Hey, why not us?"

Considerable frustration accumulated from repetitive finishes behind the Yankees in the standings. Gradually, though, it became apparent that in one way, the White Sox were definitely better than the Yankees. The Sox had a better overall fielding team. As a starting pitcher, Pierce loved to see the men arranged behind him on the diamond. He knew the opposition would get no cheap hits with Jim Landis in center, Luis Aparicio at short, Nellie Fox at second, Jim Rivera in right, and Sherm Lollar catching. Those guys were less likely to drop the ball than to let a bar of soap slip out of their hands.

"The fielding up the middle was fantastic," Pierce said. "We won the close ballgames, especially in 1959. The 1–1 games we ended up winning because we had a good solid shortstop, second baseman, and center fielder. We had such a good defensive ball-club. We didn't give away anything."

Pierce roomed on the road with second baseman Nellie Fox for 11 years, and the men were close. Pierce recalled once even teasing Fox about his throwing arm in the middle of a game.

A grounder was hit to shortstop Luis Aparicio, who flipped the ball to Fox, who completed the relay to first for a double play, though his throw had little steam on it.

"I called him over to the mound," Pierce said. "And I told him, 'If I had your change of pace, I'd be the greatest pitcher in base-ball.' He cursed at me."

Chasing Perfection

During his seasons with the White Sox, Billy Pierce threw four one-hitters without ever completing a no-hitter. One of the most memorable games of his career was the first one-hitter, partially because it came against the Yankees.

On June 15, 1950, on a damp day in Chicago, the Yankees were visiting Comiskey Park. Pierce stifled the New York bats, besting Ed Lopat and shutting out the Yanks, 5–0.

It was a game that almost did not take place. The umpires considered postponing the game because of the severe rain. There were three rain delays, the way Pierce remembers it, and he often thought the game would never be completed.

Whenever they peeled the tarp back, Pierce went out to pitch. Whenever the umpires said to play ball, he played ball. In between, he rested his left arm and figured he would never have to go nine innings. Pierce said the rain was coming down hard enough in the fourth inning that he thought likely the game was going to be terminated. At that time he was still throwing a no-hitter.

In the fifth inning, Yankees third baseman Billy Johnson stroked a clean single, the only hit of the day off Pierce. If there had been an early rainout the game would have gone into the books as incomplete. With the White Sox taking an early lead, Pierce said he wanted it to play out and to post the win against New York. Around the seventh inning, umpire Bill Summers said, "We'll finish this ballgame."

"Some of the fellows in the outfield got some pretty slushy feet in the mud out there," Pierce said. "But we did finish the game."

Some pitchers are in a zone when they throw. They just pluck those tosses back to the mound from the catcher out of the air and rear back and fire again. Others are aware of every little aspect of the game going on around them. It is supposed to be bad luck to talk to a pitcher who is throwing a no-hitter, but some pitchers are too laid-back to believe in superstition. Others know better than their fielders what is going on.

The average fan, who looks at the scoreboard almost constantly to read balls and strikes and the line score, pays more attention to the writing on the wall, but that doesn't mean the pitcher is unaware. Most major league pitchers have thrown no-hitters somewhere along the way in their career, and for them it is no big deal to be blanking a team for five or more innings. After the game passes the halfway mark, they might go, "Hmmm" and start to think about the prospects of a no-hitter.

"In that game [versus the Yankees], it was about halfway through when they got a hit, so you're not thinking about it," Pierce said. "When the White Sox played the Yankees in the 1950s, you were thinking about a victory, to get a win, because we didn't beat them that often. The White Sox were just starting to get better as a team, starting to show that we could be a contender. I was just thinking *victory*, and it turned out to be a one-hitter, which was very nice. But we had a win and had a shutout, so I was very contented, I'll tell you."

Few pitchers, Pierce among them, enter a ballgame thinking about pitching a no-hitter. If one comes along—and they are rare enough occurrences for anyone who ever pitched except for Nolan Ryan and his seven beauties—that's gravy.

"Number one, first things first, I'm going to win the game," Pierce said. "That is the only thing you think of, just really going out and winning the game. Nowadays, there's so much pitching philosophy that teams barely have the idea that the pitcher is going to finish the game, never mind pitch a no-hitter. They don't expect him to be in the game after the sixth inning most of the time. We went out there with the mindset that we were going to pitch nine innings and finish the game. It was a nine-inning game, and that's what you thought about. Even when I was playing amateur ball in Detroit we played nine innings, and so I was always used to going out there and throwing nine innings."

Pierce won 211 games in the majors and pitched 193 complete games.

Usually, the only time he ever said hello to relief pitchers was if they were all hanging out together in the clubhouse, not handing off the ball when the other guy came in from the bullpen.

The 1950 game was Pierce's first one-hitter. He also pitched a one-hitter for the Sox on April 16, 1953, beating the St. Louis Browns and Harry "the Cat" Brecheen, 1–0. On June 27, 1958, Pierce flung his third one-hitter for Chicago, beating Russ Kemmerer and the Washington Senators, 3–0. And on June 11, 1959, Pierce tossed his fourth one-hitter for the Sox, overcoming Camilo Pascual and the Senators again, this time at Griffith Stadium in Washington, D.C., 3–1.

In black and white, on paper, or talking out loud and hearing that a pitcher threw a one-hitter, it sounds as if it was a close call for a no-hitter. Pierce doesn't see it that way. The first one was not a close call because the hit came early, he said.

"I don't consider it a close call just because it was a one-hitter," Pierce said. "If it happens early in the game, the thought of a no-hitter doesn't enter your mind. There could be one play where it's a clean line drive. That's not a close call, that's a clean base hit. There was only one real close call."

During the first one-hitter against Washington in Comiskey Park, Pierce carried a no-hitter into the ninth inning of the night game. Everyone in the park was aware of the situation—fans, players, managers, and the pitcher, too. Even more delicious, Pierce was pitching a perfect game. The joint was rocking more than it would at an Elvis Presley concert.

With two outs in the ninth inning and the White Sox leading by three runs, Pierce was pitching for immortality. The Senators sent up a pinch-hitter to see if he could wage a little bit of destruction. Ed FitzGerald played 12 years in the big leagues, mostly with the Pittsburgh Pirates and the Senators. A catcher who wielded a respectable bat, FitzGerald recorded a lifetime batting average of .260. FitzGerald was known as a fastball hitter, so Pierce threw him a curveball away.

"He swung his bat and hit it over the first baseman's head for a double," Pierce said. "There went the perfect game, there went the no-hitter, and everything else. I struck out the next batter."

Game over. FitzGerald never connected safely for a more suspenseful hit.

"That's close," Pierce said.

Of his four one-hitters, Pierce thinks most often about that one, how close he came not only to a no-hitter, but to a perfect game, a pitching accomplishment posted about once every 10 years.

"That one felt a little bit different because you knew what you had going," Pierce said. "When they get the hit in the fourth, fifth, or sixth inning, then you know it's over. The pressure of a no-hitter is completely gone. Even when I was going for the perfect game the team was struggling a little bit and a win alone was important. For a long time it was 1–0. Then we made it 3–0. Most of the game I was thinking the most important thing was to win. I think in most pitchers' minds, winning the game is number one.

"Of course, if you get down to the last inning, or something like that, and you do happen to have a no-hitter, that's a different story. Then you're thinking both ways."

One of Pierce's friends was sitting in the stands watching him pitch that night, and he brought along a girlfriend who was a baseball novice. Pierce's friend was a fan who liked to keep his own box score on one of the scorecards sold at the stadium. She asked him, "How do you work this?" He spent a chunk of the game teaching his girl how to fill in the appropriate symbols.

After a while, when he noted that Pierce had neither allowed a hit, nor permitted a base runner, the guy turned to his date and said, "Now that scorebook is going to be a good scorebook to have." The game moved into the ninth inning, and Pierce set down the first two men in order before allowing the critical double to FitzGerald. The man looked at the girl, looked at FitzGerald standing on first, then looked at the scorecard and said, "Throw it away."

Camaraderie

One by one, as the White Sox roster became set after Lane's whirlwind of trading, the players became friendlier and gradually bonded. Pierce said he made several lifetime friends sharing experiences during those years. Even guys who were not exceptionally close greet one another with hugs and laughter whenever they see each other, whether it is at a reunion, a golf tournament, a White Sox game, or the White Sox's annual winter fan convention.

The kidding about "Remember the time when..." begins almost immediately. Sometimes the barbs are sharp and listeners don't understand the closeness of the men's teasing.

"As my wife, Gloria, has said many times when she hears us talking," Pierce said, 'How can you fellows do this to each other and nobody gets mad at each other? I mean you dig each other. You remember that shot that this guy hit off you or remember what you did?'"

During one period of time, Pierce was missing his best stuff and kept surrendering life-threatening line drives down the third-base line. In baseball parlance, third base is called the hot corner for that reason. Sammy Esposito was holding down the slot when a liner hit him in the leg. After Pierce asked after his health, Esposito said he was going to ask the manager to change the lineup so he would still be able to have kids some day.

Given Lane's propensity to change players for the sake of change sometimes, it was rather remarkable that a core group of White Sox stayed together and played together for most of the 1950s. Even for Lane, no matter how much his trigger finger itched, trading off All-Stars and future Hall of Famers seemed like

Pitcher Billy Pierce (left) shares a moment with friend and fellow pitcher Early Wynn prior to the All-Star Game on July 8, 1958. Scenes like this were common among the tightly knit 1950s White Sox.

bad business. So many of the guys were teammates for years. Pierce and Nellie Fox roomed together on the road for a decade. Fox, Aparicio, Pierce, and Lollar were all stalwarts, as familiar to the South Side fans as their neighbors in the next-door two-flat.

"We were very close," Pierce said of the 1950s White Sox. "Closer than fellows on teams get nowadays. It was because we roomed together. We were together all the time. You could rib each other and kid each other. A guy might strike out and someone would say, 'You looked terrible on that one.' But they would take it in a kidding way. You never saw any fights in the dugout like you do now."

The Man Who Turned It Around

Al Lopez gets the credit for leading the White Sox to the 1959 pennant, but after decades in the doldrums, the White Sox first made their move to respectability on the watch of Paul Richards between 1951 and 1954.

Lopez, a Hall of Famer and renowned strategist, and Richards were very different in their approaches to baseball teams.

"They had a different philosophy altogether," Billy Pierce said. "Al figured most players were veteran players. He liked to work more with the veteran players than the rookies. Richards was focused more on teaching. They both qualify as very good managers, no question about it. But they managed in different ways. Richards was more into the player individually, I think, and Al was into more of a team concept. He felt the players were veterans so he shouldn't have to teach them anything.

"Al could be very, very nice. He'd get excited in a ballgame, though, once in a while, but of course Richards would, too. He had more run-ins with umpires than anybody. Al hooked up with the players sometimes, too. He was a little bit on edge."

Winning helps define a manager's reputation. Pierce said the résumé makes a huge difference in how a manager is remembered. Lopez is recalled as the man who guided the two American League teams to pennants in the years the Yankees didn't win in the 1950s. Richards is best remembered in Sox lore for helping put them on the right track.

"You have to have the talent to win, and all of a sudden you turn great," Pierce said. "If you were a pitching coach and you didn't have a winning team, you weren't a great pitching coach, or you weren't a great hitting coach. The minute you do have a winning team, all of a sudden you're a genius. That's the game. People like success, and the media does, too."

Richards was a catcher born in Waxahachie, Texas in 1908. He broke into the majors with the Brooklyn Dodgers in 1932, and only once in his eight-year career did he appear in as many as 100 games in a season. He finished with a lowly .227 batting average. But Richards knew talent, he knew baseball, and he knew how to handle men. He was also regarded as something of a savant when it came to managing a pitching staff.

Billy Pierce was still in the Tigers organization when he first met Richards and Richards managed him at AAA Buffalo.

"Richards insisted to me, 'Bill, you've got to come up with a slider,'" Pierce said. "I tried all different ways he wanted me to try. I couldn't do it. Finally, one day I did something different, and I came up with a slider. It made a lot of difference in my pitching. But Paul was that type. He got an idea, and he put you to work on it. Once, he tied Chico Carrasquel into the batting cage because Chico would move one way or the other away from the plate, and Richards didn't want him to do that. He actually tied him in one place while he was taking batting practice to break the habit. Chico couldn't move his foot around."

Another time Richards was being driven batty by a lesser-known pitcher who, on the follow-through of his motion, would cross the wrong foot in front of his body. Richards dug up a broomstick and put it in front of the guy and ordered him not to cross over it.

Richards was pals with the wonderful second baseman Joe Gordon, and he brought Gordon into spring training camp to work with Nellie Fox around the second-base bag.

"He was a great teacher," Pierce said of Richards. "To me, he was the best manager I ever had. He taught. He didn't just sit back and manage. Our problem when Paul was managing us was that we didn't have the bench the Yankees had. We tried to match them player-for-player, and they just always had that extra player on us to make something happen."

If Richards's first passion was baseball, golf ran a close second.

"He loved to play golf," Pierce said. "He was a good golfer, too. One day in spring training, the pitchers are out running—we ran an awful lot. We ran and ran and ran. Paul said, 'Bill, you guys keep running. I'm going inside for a minute.'"

The pitchers followed orders and kept running and running until they thought they might be in training for the Boston Marathon instead of Opening Day. They ran for 45 more minutes before Richards's psyche job dawned on Pierce.

"I'm figuring that I know where he's gone," Pierce said. "He's gone golfing, and he just wants to see how long we'll run. What should we do? I said, 'Let's run another 10 minutes and that's it.' We ran and went into the clubhouse. The next day Paul came up to me, and I looked at him, and he said, 'How long did you run before you knew that I wouldn't be back?' I told him we ran for about an hour, but we didn't mind, we were used to it. 'But you could have at least told us what you were going to do. What'd you shoot?'"

Richards's chuckling response was, "I did rather well."

Waking Up the Fans

Those who followed baseball in the 1930s and 1940s would be amazed that major league teams in some cities are drawing more than 3 million fans per season. Before 1950, a good year for the White Sox at Old Comiskey Park was in the 800,000 range.

In 1955, after the Sox had fielded a good product for a few years in a row, the team drew a record attendance of 1.6 million fans. Don't think the players didn't notice the upsurge in enthusiasm, either.

"The crowds were changing from 7,000 to 20,000 a game, and when we played the Yankees on a weekend we drew 50,000 [four times there were 52,000 or more fans when the Sox played New York in the early 1950s]," Pierce said. "The tremendous fan interest helped the ballplayers. They had been used to playing in front of a few. Now they had all these people pulling for them, and it was just great. The team's attitude changed. It was no longer, 'Let's just keep it close.' Or, 'Let's just not let this team pound us.' When our hitters came along we could battle Boston and New York and Cleveland.

"You get the feeling. Without question you could feel that you had a chance to win every ballgame. When you got behind a run, well, the game wasn't over yet. We can catch up, you know. It wasn't a feeling that the other team was going to get us now. We were going to get them. This was a team that did not give up. They kept playing hard at all times. We didn't have eight or nine super-stars. We had good ballplayers, *real* good players."

Many championship teams have adopted a theme for their season, but the White Sox not only established the Go-Go White Sox in 1951, they made it endure. Bumper stickers were printed that first year touting the theme. The "Go-Go Sox" song came along. The image stuck and was popular.

After a few years on the upswing, fans started to fill the building and take an additional interest beyond attendance. They brought their children up as White Sox fans and kids started their own fan clubs boosting individual players. There was a Nellie Fox fan club, a Jim Rivera fan club, a Jim Landis fan club, a Billy Pierce fan club.

"There were at least five or six different groups of kids with fan clubs," Pierce said.

Most of the kids were between 14 and 16 years old, to Pierce's recollection, a majority of them somewhat surprisingly being girls, but also boys.

"The Billy Pierce fan club was called the Strikeouts," the pitcher said. "It seemed they were mainly girls. The families would invite us over to dinner. My wife and I went over for dinner to the president's house. When Gloria and I were having our first child, the parents of the president called my mother and my wife's mother to come over for a shower for Gloria. This type of thing happened. It was very big. Nellie had a really big fan club. You don't see anything like that now."

One of the boys in the Strikeouts became a lifelong Pierce friend. They met through the fan club, and later the young man became a priest. Billy and Gloria Pierce attended when he was ordained, and the couple and the priest are still in touch.

"We still communicate at Christmas with him," Pierce said.

chapter 7
Old Sportshirt

Sox Owner Bill Veeck was a fun-loving showman who approached life and baseball with a smile on his face.

Veeck—as in Laughs

The greatest fan-friendly baseball-team owner in history invented the exploding scoreboard, installed a fan shower in the outfield seats for cooling off on hot summer days, and introduced names on the back of jerseys.

Bill Veeck took over the Chicago White Sox from the descendants of Charles A. Comiskey, supervised winning a pennant in 1959, sold the team, and later reacquired it. Veeck refused to wear a tie to even the most formal of occasions, so for years *The Sporting News* referred to him in headlines as "Sportshirt" rather than by name. Given the stuffiness of the other owners and the formality of their wardrobes, no one wondered who was being talked about.

The more casual approach to attire symbolized the type of man Veeck was. He may have hobnobbed with moneymen and was a member of a millionaires' club of baseball-team owners, but he wasn't of their stripe—or their striped suits. He was a man of the people who grew up in the game as a youngster romping through Wrigley Field while his dad, William, ran the franchise from 1919 to 1933. He never lost his common touch or forgot he was a fan first, and above all he held onto the childish impulse to put having a good time ahead of most other pursuits. Making sure spectators had fun at the ballpark—that they would go home and tell their friends about the unexpected pleasures that accompanied the game—ran neck-and-neck with winning for Veeck. Yes, ideally, every team he governed would win the World Series, but he was not above throwing up smokescreens to make sure the fans wouldn't dwell on losing if the team couldn't finish on the north side of .500.

The man who sent midget Eddie Gaedel up to bat when he was running the St. Louis Browns, and who oversaw the Cleveland Indians as they broke attendance records (2.6 million fans) and won the 1948 World Series, was a showman, a promoter, the P.T. Barnum of baseball. He had a twinkle in his eye and a grin on his face whenever he wasn't slowed down by any of the myriad injuries and illnesses that afflicted him. Veeck wore a wooden leg as a souvenir of a World War II wound, but he had an ashtray built into it so he had a place to flick his cigarette detritus. He was bold, brazen, and brash and avoided playing political games—sometimes to his own detriment. Veeck loved to tweak the establishment, because the establishment abhorred him, and he liked to make those proper fellows nervous.

As did many affiliated with other American League clubs, Veeck hated the Yankees. But whereas most would just mumble their distaste for the juggernaut under their breaths, Veeck would shout his feelings from the tallest skyscraper in Chicago.

He publicly referred to Yankees general manager George Weiss as "one of my least favorite people" because "Mr. Weiss is completely devoid of a sense of humor and the milk of human kindness. I suppose a good part of my antipathy to him is jealousy. The fellow is the best operator in baseball, but cold fish always irritate me. It's fun to deflate and annoy them. The madder they get, the more fun you can have with them."

Weiss did not invite Veeck over for martinis at the cocktail hour.

A passionate baseball man, Veeck endeared himself to the hourly laborer with such promotions as Ladies Day and Good Old Joe Early Night, honoring an everyday fan. He wanted fans to show up at Comiskey Park not only to see the Go-Go White Sox prevail, but to get a laugh, a story to tell, or a memory that would stick.

In Cleveland Veeck brought the first African American player to the American League—Larry Doby, a few months after Jackie Robinson broke the color barrier—and hired 42-year-old relief pitcher Satchel Paige, not as a charity cause, but because he recognized that the man could still pitch.

Veeck grew up in baseball, and upon the orders of P.K. Wrigley, he put the famous ivy up on the outfield walls at Wrigley Field in the 1930s. By the late 1950s, Veeck had been out of baseball for five seasons and wanted back in. Through creative financing (since he did not have significant cash of his own),

Veeck put together a partnership to buy the White Sox. The team had been in the Comiskey family since Charles brought it to Chicago from St. Paul some 58 years earlier. But the children of Grace Comiskey were fighting over ownership. Veeck swooped in and bought 54 percent of the stock for $2.7 million.

Veeck, his reddish-blondish hair in curls (sportswriters called him burr head or even frizzletop), his unconscious maneuvering with the stump of his injured leg, was every man's pal if they wanted to have fun shooting the bull about baseball, basking in the bleachers, or sharing beers in the Bard's Room at Comiskey Park. No one wanted to win pennants as much as Veeck, but the difference between Veeck and other owners was that he could appreciate small victories. A team could be bad, dropping far in the standings, but business could be good if fans still kept turning out.

"This may be heresy, but most people are not basically interested in the technique of baseball," Veeck said. "They are casual fans who want fun and excitement. I can't guarantee every game will be exciting. Nobody can. There are bound to be very dull 11–2 games that are boring no matter which side you root for. But I can provide my fans with entertaining fun."

Veeck was a voracious reader, and he possessed a keen intellect. But he was no snob. The thinking of the day was that football was the college man's game. Veeck was willing to concede the gridiron to these so-called thinkers, but he chose to claim the working-class fan for himself.

"Baseball serves the identical purpose for the working man," Veeck said. "It gives him an emotional outlet, an excuse for yelling harmless insults at the umpires and the visiting team, and for knocking off a few cans of beer. Maybe the home team gets murdered, and he can't sound off. So I create a gala atmosphere, give him something to talk about, with fireworks, bands, pretty girls, and even midgets."

It always came back to the midget. Pinch-hitter Gaedel, who stood 3'7", was ordered to step into the batter's box in his mini Browns uniform during a game in 1951, take four pitches, and walk to first. Veeck threatened Gaedel that if he so much as took his Louisville slugger off his shoulder, the owner would kill him. Gaedel crouched at the plate, making his strike zone "no bigger than a postage stamp." He walked on four pitches, and a chuckling Veeck, who weathered accusations that he was making a travesty of the game, said he was certain the incident would be highly played in his obituaries when he died.

"When you can't laugh at yourself, you're in real trouble," Veeck said.

The American Way

Even though Bill Veeck felt he purchased the White Sox fair and square, he ended up in court defending his deal from a disappointed, angry, and infuriated Chuck Comiskey, team vice president and son of the previous owner. Comiskey wanted the team for himself and couldn't believe when he was outmaneuvered and left with the 46 percent minority shares his mother had willed him. He was mightily ticked off when his sister, Dorothy Rigney, agreed to sell her majority shares to Veeck in March 1959. Veeck had moved to exercise a previously staked-out option on February 17. For Comiskey it was a case of "When in a hopeless position, sue. When in doubt, sue. When you are out of options, sue."

Veeck—who needed to acquire more shares to establish the board of directors—extended an olive branch to young Comiskey, offering to work with him and keep him involved.

"We are hoping for an amicable and friendly solution that will be for the best interests of everyone," Veeck said. "We'd like to have Chuck join us as a partner and keep the Comiskey name up front in Chicago baseball."

Comiskey opted for the Patrick Henry approach—give me the White Sox, or give me death. Veeck said he envisioned a White Sox organization where he was president of the team and Comiskey was chairman of the board. Comiskey envisioned a team where Veeck would have to pay scalpers to buy a ticket to get in the door of the stadium named after his grandfather.

"He can't be mad at me for buying his sister's stock, because if I hadn't somebody else would have," Veeck said. "What's the difference?"

Perhaps that was the point. Maybe Comiskey didn't differentiate Veeck from any other buyer. All Comiskey knew was that his hold on the team was going down the drain fast, quicker with every court appearance. Not that the realization came easily or smoothly. In Tampa, Florida, where the White Sox were gathering for spring training, a reporter asked Comiskey who was in charge of the team. "I am," he replied forcefully. But he wasn't.

Veeck, who by all legal authority was inching towards formally being named president, made no such dictatorial pronouncements. With a straight face, in an attempt to be conciliatory, he said, "I'm just here as a spectator."

Veeck told reporters that in his first week after sealing the deal to buy the Sox, he made six speeches on behalf of the club to jump-start interest in the 1959 campaign, and he said he had 90 more engagements scheduled. That was Veeck, a politician on the road, the king of rubber-chicken dinners who would go anywhere to plug his ball team.

"If we want fans to come from Rock Island to see our games," Veeck said of the community on the Iowa border, about 120 miles from Chicago, "we should be willing to go there. After all, it's no farther from Chicago to Rock Island than it is from Rock Island to Chicago. I'm a great believer in the personal touch."

Veeck had owned two major league teams and a minor league club in Milwaukee and had made failed attempts to purchase the Washington Senators, Pittsburgh Pirates, and Detroit Tigers, but he had always dreamed of owning one of Chicago's teams. For him, the transaction was a dream come true. For Comiskey, who wanted to keep the team in his family for a couple more generations, it was a nightmare.

It had taken a couple of years for Veeck, approaching Dorothy Rigney through her husband, John, team vice president, to convince her to sell. In the beginning, even when she would barely talk about such an idea, she said her inclination was to sell her shares to her brother, if anyone. It took most of a year to budge Rigney off the fence.

Although Walter O'Malley had staked out Los Angeles as prime territory when he moved the Brooklyn Dodgers west, there were rumors the White Sox might join the National League club overlooking the Pacific Ocean. The propositon was one of the first things Veeck was asked, and he instantly and vehemently denied it.

"Chicago is my hometown," Veeck said. "I'm coming home and glad of it. My one goal is to develop a winner in Chicago. I haven't the slightest notion of moving the franchise."

It was hard to picture any moving trucks loaded with Luke Appling's old spikes or Ted Lyons's old glove heading off into the night to another city. It was a considerably different situation when Veeck proposed moving the St. Louis Browns to Baltimore six years earlier. The Browns were doomed. The Cardinals owned the town. American League owners refused to let Veeck move as a way to run him out of their fraternity. Then they promptly voted to allow another ownership group to do the same thing. Thus were born the Baltimore Orioles.

Veeck did not seem like the type to move one of the teams of his youth. He was too much the Chicagoan, and he had too much belief in his ability to make any team a financial success with promotions to even worry about why a move would be needed.

During his years away from baseball, Veeck remained a nerve-racking thorn in the side of the game, egging on owners in interviews and authoring a multi-part syndicated newspaper series in August 1958 titled "I Know Who's Killing Baseball." It was a flurry of torpedo shots at the owners for being dull and unimaginative.

Once wound up, Veeck could talk forever, and talking about the ills of the game he loved wound him up tighter and louder than any other subject. Of course none of this made him any new friends among other owners, who had to resent someone they had basically expelled from their club for going high and mighty on them and dismissing them as dolts. Veeck was telling the world he could run their businesses better than they did.

Oh, boy, Veeck let the good-old-boys club have it.

"A one-time Brooklyn Dodger—no, not Walter O'Malley—made history after a tough day by crying out in anguish, 'In baseball, it's every man for theirself!'" Veeck wrote.

"His credo was as bad as his grammar. But unfortunately, it's the guiding philosophy of most big-league club owners. And it has brought the sport to its present peril, a few short years from disaster."

That was, unless the baseball owners whom he deemed to be selfish and greedy listened to Bill Veeck and adopted his ideas and plans. For starters, he said, the richest teams controlled too many young players on their minor league teams and drafted too many choice players. He sought more player availability for the have-nots through an unrestricted draft.

Tied in with that thinking, Veeck advocated eliminating the farm system where the richest teams stashed players and kept them in the minors rather than bringing them to the parent roster, or in the case of players who couldn't make the team, allowing them to go to other major league teams.

"Who needs farm systems?" Veeck asked.

Veeck proposed doing away with individual team scouts and combining scouting under a major league pool. He suggested subsidizing the entire minor league system. He urged television contracts to be written so that free major league games were not piped into minor league towns on the days of local games and that visiting teams got a share of home TV profits.

The once and future owner reiterated his idea that baseball should be sold to the masses as a form of entertainment, rather than as the national pastime handed down as if it were played due to the divine right of kings who only periodically allowed the commoners to head out to the park.

"Some of baseball's biggest woes," Veeck said, "are due to the fact that it has always been sold on the basis of the won-and-lost columns rather than as a delightful form of entertainment. It's a universal trait, I suppose, to identify yourself with a winner and shun a loser. It's a trait that can't be discarded overnight, and conditions being what they are in the American League, how can you expect the fans in seven cities in that league to support their teams when the Yankees have the pennant sewed up by Mother's Day?"

What Veeck wanted baseball to do, he said, was "dress up an otherwise drab presentation with entertainment that gives, or at least tries to give, the fans their money's worth even though the ballclub of their hearts is 20 games back of the Yanks."

Rather humorously, as if he was the main man who should sound off on Veeck's baseball dissertation, a day later Federal Bureau of Investigation director J. Edgar Hoover chimed in with his thoughts. For those in the hierarchy of baseball ownership who might have thought the nation's chief cop and enforcer would duly dismiss Veeck's demolition of the farm system and dumping of a strictly run draft as Bolshevism, Hoover did not in any way think of Veeck as a Commie.

"It makes good, sound sense to me for all of the major league clubs to pool their resources and have their scouts recommend young baseball talent for a common draft," Hoover said of Veeck's multifaceted save-baseball plan. "Competition—fair, open, and vigorous—is the backbone of our American system. It is what we call free enterprise, and there should be no place for monopoly in sports any more than any other business."

It sounded as if the head G-man, like so many other fans, might be a frustrated Washington Senators rooter who was sick of the New York Yankees winning all of the time.

Practice What You Preach

All of a sudden—or so it must have seemed to those steamed owners—Bill Veeck was one of them again, the owner of his third major league team and prepared to unleash his promotional genius again.

It should be remembered that Veeck's wizardry was probably in his genes. His father, William, is the one who correctly foresaw the popularity of Ladies Day. He taught his son to always respect the paying customer. From the time he was 14, young Bill worked various jobs at Wrigley Field and absorbed all aspects of behind-the-scenes operations and what made a baseball team tick.

As a teenager Veeck sold tickets, worked in the concessions department's stock room, worked as a vendor, worked with the grounds crew, and worked in the front office. When the younger Veeck was about to assume the reins of the White Sox, he told an interviewer a story about how one day his father took him into the cashier's office and showed him the day's receipts.

"I want you to remember one thing about that money," Veeck remembered his father telling him. "It's all one color—you can't tell who gave it to you."

The lesson was that all people's money was created equally—the big shots in the fancy box seats and the less wealthy in the bleacher seats, men and women, boys and girls, whites and blacks. They were all baseball fans to be respected.

Veeck was determined to make new friends and create new White Sox fans when he took over the team's operations. In the endless pursuit of fresh fans, Veeck wooed mothers, or as one contemporary account reported in May 1959 after Mother's Day, Veeck was "a favorite son."

The stereotype of mothers being rewarded on their special annual day involves being fed breakfast in bed by the kids, having their whims catered to by hubbies, and the choosing of the day's family entertainment left solely to their discretion. Veeck tempted the mothers by introducing a White Sox home game as a pre-ferred selection for the day's activity. He announced that all mothers would be admitted for free to Comiskey Park's double-header against the Cleveland Indians provided they brought a picture of their children. Most of the women arrived bearing wallet-sized photos of Junior and Jeannette. However, one mom, who said she didn't have any small pictures of her kids, showed up carrying a poster-sized photo of her children. The splashy picture—almost as tall as she was—earned her an audience with Veeck.

For one day Veeck was the world's foremost expert on orchids, too, eclipsing the interest of eccentric fictional detective Nero Wolfe by ordering 10,000 orchids in miniature. The snooty Wolfe, naturally, would not bother himself with an "inferior" product, but Veeck was trying to make a statement more than cornering the market. And he was on a budget.

"It's not the size of the orchids that counts," Veeck said, "but the sentiment."

As if free admission and flowers were not enough, Veeck offered many other prizes to the ladies. He strove to make the day one of the most memorable of their lives and to sell them on White Sox baseball permanently.

Among the gifts given to the moms were 1,000 bottles of root beer, 1,000 pies, 1,000 cupcakes, 100 cans of beer, 100 free dinners at a Chicago restaurant, and tickets for two to all 21 of the team's night games for the rest of the season, with the additional bonus of paid babysitting.

"The White Sox have the smallest attendance of females of any major league team," Veeck said. "It's in our interest to arouse interest by the ladies."

When the accountants figured the impact of the promotion, it was realized that 3,947 mothers took advantage of the offer and claimed free tickets. A sampling of the mothers interviewed on that day gushed with compliments for Bill Veeck. A woman named Pat Howell from suburban Forest Park sounded as if she was ready to adopt Veeck.

"I love him," she said. "He's a good salesman. He makes you feel like you're welcome. With Bill Veeck, we'll go right into first place."

It's always hard to measure the long-term value of such a promotion. Did all of those women who came for free batter down the gates in the future to pay for tickets? Who knows? Veeck definitely made them feel good on Mother's Day, though.

Although he loved baseball, loved showmanship, and wanted to win, Veeck did try to avoid the worst trait of sports-team owners and racehorse owners. The first rule of self-preservation is not to fall in love with the merchandise. Racehorse owners who make the mistake of falling for a losing horse because it is pretty and looks like a winner are legion. It's more complicated in baseball because the contestants are human beings. Veeck was too gregarious to fit the mold of the dispassionate owner, and in some instances he became lifelong friends with players, always reaching out to them in one capacity or another during his travels to bring them back into his fold.

Outfielder Larry Doby, the man Veeck hired to break the color line in the American League when both were with the Indians, later played for the White Sox, and much later Veeck made Doby the second black manager in baseball history.

Minnie Minoso and Veeck also had a special relationship. Not only was Minoso a superior ballplayer in the outfield and a devoted White Sox player, he also had the spirit to participate in one of Veeck's most fulfilling projects. Minoso kept himself in shape even after retiring in 1964 from a long career in the majors. Veeck brought Minoso back to active duty as a designated hitter for a few games in 1976 and 1980, making him a five-decade player. Later, Mike Veeck, the third-generation baseball front-office executive, activated Minoso in the independent minor leagues, allowing him to play in the 1990s and 2000s.

Minoso, now in his 80s, is unlikely to go for another decade, but he is proud that the Veecks helped him attain the unique status of a seven-decade player, and he wears a special ring to commemorate the achievement.

The Mother's Day bash was a major showcase treat on the schedule, but Veeck did not discriminate against other groups. If he could think of a worthy tie-in, he welcomed a subculture to the ballpark with fanfare. Besides the moms, Veeck designated free admission days for bartenders and cab drivers—whenever they could get off from their jobs on the night shift. The White Sox celebrated National Dairy Day right alongside the industry by allowing barnyard animals to parade on the field between games of a doubleheader. Some fans might have wanted to boo, but the cows wanted to moo.

The cows were not the only livestock, even though their presence did make the most sense. There were also burros, pigs, ducks, chickens, and horses, leading some to wonder just what the menagerie all had to do with dairy products. Veeck just said cheese—and smiled. Even more bizarre, star pitcher Early Wynn participated as an anonymous horse rider subsequently unmasked. The Lone Ranger! Wynn and other White Sox players then went head-to-head and hand-to-hand in a milking contest. Hard to imagine today's players volunteering unless they grew up on the farm.

Proving that he would be receptive to just about any weird idea if it created attention for the White Sox, during his first season at the helm Veeck signed off on an airline company gimmick promoting flights to a new destination. A helicopter landed in the Comiskey Park infield and space-suited Martian midgets (it was never clear if Eddie Gaedel was going for more fame or not) emerged and pretended to kidnap Sox shortstop Luis Aparicio and second baseman Nellie Fox, who were not much taller than the invaders.

Veeck probably figured if one midget became a nationwide phenomenon, then a handful of midgets would take the White Sox intergalactic.

chapter 8

Throwing Piercing Stuff

Billy Pierce (right), one of the best pitchers ever to grace the White Sox, receives pitching tips from veteran Sox player Big Ed Walsh.
Photo courtesy of AP/World Wide Photos.

The Little Left-Hander

The Go-Go White Sox featured little guys. There was Little Looie at shortstop and Little Nel at second base and the Little Left-Hander, Billy Pierce, on the pitcher's mound every fourth day. Pierce stood 5'10" and weighed 160 pounds or so but figured he threw about 92 mph when his fastball was hopping.

Athletes are bigger in the 2000s than they were in the 1950s, but the Sox were undersized at many spots even by the standards of the time. That's why their game relied more on speed than power. Except in the cases of the very short, an Albie Pearson, or a little bit later, Fred Patek, there was less preoccupation with the physical dimensions of a player than with the tools he possessed to do the job.

In the 1950s starting pitchers threw more innings than their counterparts do in the 2000s, yet as a rule they struck out fewer batters. Surprisingly to some, Pierce led the American League in strikeouts in 1953 with 186. Yet he also pitched 271⅓ innings, far more than pitchers throw today. More tellingly, Pierce led the American League in complete games in 1956 with 21, in 1957 with 16, and in 1958 with 19. Those would be unheard-of numbers today when some starters cruise through the season without throwing a complete game at all.

In two of his better accomplishments, Pierce led the league in victories with 20 in 1957, and in 1955 he led the league in earned-run average with a 1.97 mark. It was the lowest ERA in the majors since 1946. Around that time the New York Yankees tried to trade for Pierce. Culmination of such a trade would have likely rewritten history. The move would have put Pierce and Ford, two dominating southpaws, in the same rotation. It also probably would have weakened the White Sox just enough that they wouldn't have captured the 1959 flag.

Pierce had excellent control. When he began his windup, his left, or throwing, hand was behind his head, and when he swung around to complete his delivery the ball came in an arc from over his shoulder. He never looked as if he was straining his muscles, never appeared to be working hard with his throws. His motion was effortless and clean, with no herky-jerky moves.

The young pitcher suffered his growing pains with the Tigers and in his first season or so with the White Sox, but by 1951 he was beginning to gain recognition as a thrower to be feared. A *Sporting News* story cemented his reputation. It read in part, "When Billy Pierce has his stuff, there is no pitcher in the land who is so good. This is the judgment of many sound hitters who have been mystified by the artistry of the young lefty of the White Sox, who just turned 24 on April 2. The dark-eyed little southpaw right now probably would bring $250,000 if he were suddenly tossed on the open market. And he'd be worth every penny of it."

Pierce had been a high school ace in Detroit and had professional scouts watching him when he was only 15. However, as is proven over and over again, early achievement does not guarantee instant success at a higher level. Number one draft picks go bust all the time. Late bloomers arrive on the radar screen after every team has given up on them.

In 1945 Pierce's record with Buffalo was only 5–7. The next year he had a bad back and finished 3–4. Early promise was leading to questions like "What's up?" in the Detroit front office. And eventually Pierce's struggles made him expendable and led to his being traded to the White Sox.

One reason Pierce praises old manager Paul Richards so enthusiastically now is the way Richards treated him in the minors when his body was aching and his mind was at loose ends.

"Paul nursed me along carefully," Pierce said. "He didn't work me too much for fear my back trouble would return. He kept stressing control over everything else. Paul was a wonderful manager for me. He had my future at heart. In fact, he would catch me most of the time. In two games, he even caught me despite the fact that he had a broken finger."

Richards's patience paid off for both men only a few years later after Pierce was traded from the Tigers to Chicago, and Richards was named manager of the Sox. Richards also influenced Pierce early in his career by admonishing the pitcher to slow down between throws. Pierce would catch the ball from his catcher and rush into his windup. Richards felt Pierce would be more effective if he paused a little bit longer. The message did not seem to seep through to Pierce, though.

Eventually, Richards figured out his own solution. Pierce threw a pitch, and instead of quickly returning the ball to the mound, Richards hung onto it, counted the stitches, looked for smudges, and finally zipped it back to Pierce, now antsy to go. Only he still couldn't throw because Richards was stretching, not in a squat, counting the stitches on his mitt, all before he finally gave Pierce a sign.

"I soon got the idea," Pierce said. "Once I'd controlled my overeagerness and paced myself better, I was able to control the ball."

Pierce has always been regarded as a prince of a person, and if that cost him in any way during his career it was because he didn't like to throw brushback pitches to dug-in batters. Once, in a game against the Philadelphia A's, the situation screamed out for a warning shot across Cass Michaels's bow. Pierce did not come inside, and, later, his general manager, Frank Lane, asked why not. Pierce said he didn't whip a fastball under Michaels's chin because they used to bowl together.

"They always criticized me," Pierce said, "but it just wasn't the way I played the game."

Pierce played to win, but he didn't always have luck on his side. During the 1955 season, the first time there was no 20-game winner in American League history, Pierce finished with a 15–10 record. On the surface, especially recalling Pierce's definition of a close call when seeking a no-hitter, the final mark wasn't even close to 20. However, Pierce lost four 1–0 games that season and a 3–2 game. With a little bit more hitting support Pierce would have reached the milestone.

Arthur Daley, the *New York Times* Pulitzer Prize–winning sports columnist, took note of the situation, observing, "Billy Pierce of the White Sox might have made it, but he apparently went to such extremes as walking under ladders, breaking mirrors, letting black cats cross his path, and hanging up horseshoes upside down so that the luck ran out of them."

That was the season, too, of Pierce's 1.97 earned-run average, so he clearly deserved better results. Unfortunately for him, whenever he took the mound that season the White Sox resembled those long-ago Hitless Wonders. Still, during the course of his career, Pierce ended up 42 games over .500, so he made up for the lean hitting years with fair-enough support.

Even in 1959, when manager Al Lopez was going around predicting that his club could finally overtake the Yankees, the White Sox did not have an abundance of big bats. They were renowned for their fielding and possessed the necessary pitching, but there was a shortage of power-hitting. Owner Bill Veeck and his minions searched all season long, ran up huge phone bills, but couldn't put together a trade to find that one additional big bat. Until August 25, when the White Sox acquired Ted Kluszewski from the Pittsburgh Pirates.

Given that he cost the club almost nothing, Big Klu was one of the greatest acquisitions in team history. He was local, too,

Powerful slugger Ted Kluszewski sports his trademark cut-off jersey sleeves during the 1959 World Series.

growing up in Argo, Illinois. The 230-pound slugger was a power-ful man whose trademark was cut-off jersey sleeves, the better for fans to see his bulging biceps. A four-time National League All-Star, Kluszewski led the National League in home runs with 49 and RBIs with 141, in 1954, and the next year blasted 47 more homers. He was showing signs of age and was slowing down when the White Sox picked him up for the American League stretch run, but he was the missing ingredient in the batting order.

"He gave us a big lift," Pierce said. "That extra bat in the lineup, especially a left-handed bat, meant a lot. If you look at the record, he didn't hit that many home runs for us during the regular season. But he hit some singles and doubles and knocked in runs that won games. I remember especially him doing it against Cleveland in some big games. Having the bat in the lineup meant a lot because he was a good one. There was no question about it, the other teams had to be careful."

Kluszewski hit only two home runs in the 31 regular-season games he appeared in for the Sox, but he batted .297. It was the addition of another .300 hitter who possessed long-ball threat that altered opponents' pitching strategy and boosted the Sox into pennant position. So Klu's return on expenditure was an extraordinary value.

"I don't know if we would have won the pennant without him," Pierce said.

Billy's Other Favorite Sport

Reading the headline of a first-person story written by Billy Pierce that appeared in 1956 is bound to make a baseball fan blink in disbelief. It reads, "I Love Baseball—but Bowling Is More Fun."

That's Billy Pierce's dirty little secret. The All-Star pitcher admit-ted that it would be easier and more fun to be a professional bowler. The story harkens back to Pierce's comment about how he didn't want to deliver chin music to a fellow bowler who played for the A's. Pierce was an excellent bowler. He carried a 180 average without practicing nearly as much as he would have if he had become a member of the Professional Bowlers Association and gone on tour.

This is how Pierce began his essay: "More Americans participate in bowling than in any other sport except swimming. Millions love the game, yet when I told a bowler recently that it gives me a bigger kick than pitching in the big leagues, he told me I must be kidding. I was telling the truth."

There is no written record of how Al Lopez reacted to the comment, however.

For about 1,000 words, Pierce went on to explain contrasts, differences, and similarities between bowling and baseball. Whenever he pitched a full game, Pierce said, he might lose seven pounds. Whenever he bowled, he added, he might not drop more than an ounce or two. "You obviously don't have to work as hard to roll a ball down a lane as you do to pitch to batters like Ted Williams and Mickey Mantle," Pierce wrote.

Playing baseball, Pierce said, there was always a risk of injury. In bowling, the worst damage suffered likely would be a blister on the thumb. The clock ticks fast in baseball, where players are past their prime at 35, but a bowler can keep up his good work much longer. Baseball players must sweat and work out and condition hard to excel at the sport, whereas bowlers can get by with much less "grinding work."

Pierce noted that a human being can be much more comfortable competing in bowling than in pitching when weather conspires against him.

"I've pitched when the temperature was near 40 degrees and when it was over 110 degrees on the playing fields," Pierce said. "I've pitched during windstorms, heavy drizzles, and in chilling fogs. But when I'm bowling—indoors, of course—I'm warm when a blizzard's howling outside, cool when a heat wave is scorching the streets. Being comfortable while you're competing always makes a sport more fun."

Another reason Pierce advocated the pleasures of bowling was that he could participate in the activity with his wife, Gloria, and their children. He also compared bowling to bicycling—that once learned, you never forget how to do it. There was one problem, he lamented. The White Sox worried that he would throw his arm out bowling too much, so they frowned on the potential overuse.

"Since the White Sox worry that I might strain my arm during the baseball season," Pierce wrote, "I have to lay off during the summer."

Winning the Pennant

As it did every season in the 1950s, the American League girded for another run by the Yankees at the start of the 1959 season. Only this was one of those rare off-years suffered by the Bronx Bombers during the primes of Mickey Mantle, Yogi Berra, and Whitey Ford. The White Sox had been gunning for a pennant the entire decade, but the chief foe turned out to be the Cleveland Indians, not New York.

The race was slow to unfold. All eight teams stayed within hailing distance of the top into June. Gradually the White Sox and Indians separated themselves from the pack. The Yankees finished 15 games out of first place that season. The White Sox put the finishing touches on Cleveland in late summer and won the pennant by five games. The Sox took 15 out of 22 games from the Tribe that year and that included a four-game, late-August sweep in Cleveland. It was a message series, severely wounding the Indians' hopes. Fittingly, on September 22, again in Cleveland, a White Sox victory clinched the pennant. Stalwart starter Early Wynn won his 21st game and Gerry Staley completed the game with his 15th save after Bob Shaw served as a bridge between the other two twirlers.

Billy Pierce was warming up in the bullpen in the ninth inning when Staley polished off the Indians with one pitch. Tito Francona, a left-handed hitter, was on deck, and Lopez was ready to use the left-handed Pierce in relief to gain an advantage, if necessary. It was not necessary.

"There was one out, and Vic Power was at the plate," Pierce said. "They had the bases loaded. It was a two-run ballgame

(4-2). Staley threw a sinker, and a grounder goes to Luis at short. Luis steps on second base, throws to first, and it's all over. The elation was tremendous. There was champagne and just a tremendous amount of excitement in the clubhouse."

Many of the White Sox players had been teammates for years, aspiring to experience just such a moment for most of their careers.

"To have that moment," Pierce said, "that we won, that we were the winners, was so special."

That was the night the air raid sirens went off in Chicago, creating a surreal scene to welcome the players back at Midway Airport. Mayor Richard Daley's administration had authorized the sounding of the sirens in celebration, but the general populace did not know what was happening. At the height of the Cold War, some thought an invasion by the Russians was imminent.

Enough White Sox fans got the message, however. Some estimates of the fan turnout at Midway Airport went as high as 50,000. They did not all rush to the airport, though. Many happy fans simply stepped outside their homes and set off fireworks, yelled to neighbors, or broke out the beers for a midweek party.

When the team landed and the players extricated themselves from the mob, Pierce said he and first baseman Earl Torgeson sought a taxicab. It took them a while to get a ride, and when the cab passed Garfield Boulevard, Pierce said they saw lawns lit up with flares. Fans were sitting outside their homes at 3 AM, just taking in the scene and celebrating the big victory. It was the White Sox's first pennant in 40 years, or since the Black Sox Scandal of 1919.

"The sirens woke them up," Pierce said. "But they put those flares out and were just enjoying the excitement. And it sunk in for us, too, the players. We were going to the World Series. I had been in Chicago for 10 years. I was lucky. I had been to the World Series with Detroit, but I hadn't really been a member of the team.

"In 1945 all I did was throw batting practice for Detroit. But for the White Sox, I had been part of it all the way as we built the team. To know we were going to the World Series was as exciting a time as I ever had."

chapter 9

Cy Young Reincarnated

Early Wynn (front) was the most important pitcher, and perhaps the most important player, on the 1959 pennant-winning Sox team.

The Man of the Hour

For all of the great players who populated the White Sox lineup as they struggled from disaster to respectability to strong contention during the 1950s, no single player was more important to the team's success when it won the pennant in 1959 than right-handed pitcher Early Wynn.

He looked bigger than his 6' and 200 pounds, and Wynn was strong and could be as mean as a rattlesnake if a bold batter tried to dig his spikes an inch into the batter's box. Wynn, whose nickname was Gus, broke into the majors in 1939 with the Washington Senators and won 23 games for the 111-victory Cleveland Indians of 1954.

By 1958, however, when Wynn came over to the White Sox, he was 38, and few expected him to be much of a factor in the rotation during the waning days of his career. When Wynn recorded a 14–16 mark in 1958, there was no reason for Chicago fans to look at him as a savior. Maybe he had one more year in him as a member of a first-rate rotation. But outside of Wynn's immediate family, no one would have predicted he would be the most important pitcher on the team—the most important *player* on the team—during the 1959 season.

It had long been Wynn's goal to become one of the elite pitchers in major league history by winning 300 games. Yet most baseball experts figured time had passed him by, that the 300-win ship had sailed without him.

What naysayers had not figured on was that the same will and determination that had carried Wynn for so long still coursed strongly through his body. They didn't reckon on the heart pulsing in his chest or the same spirit remaining so keen in old athletic age as it had been when he was a little bit younger and told reporters that he would throw at his mother if she crowded the plate.

Managers loved that kind of hard-nosed attitude. The statement was the most memorable of Wynn's career, though there have been variations. Some reported that he said he would throw at his grandmother. Others said he applied the same approach to his son. Regardless, the point was made: You don't dig in on Early Wynn or you'll be spinning into the dirt to avoid the fastball zipping past your ear.

Wynn was born in 1920 in Hartford, Alabama, and his childhood was marked by poverty. Becoming a big leaguer transformed his lifestyle to upper-middle class. He remembered well the youth that shaped his outlook, and he did not take kindly to any threat that would force him out of baseball. He wanted to walk away on his own terms.

"He was an individual," recalled teammate and fellow pitcher Gerry Staley. "He was sociable enough, but he went his own way. I don't think anybody went out with him much. He went his way. He had an image of a tough guy, and he was able to move the ball around out there to let the batter know who was boss. In those days you could throw at somebody, and the umpires never said anything. Now you come close with one pitch and they want to throw you out of the game. You had to like it better back then if you were a pitcher. If somebody hit a home run, they knew their next time up they were going to go down. It was understood that was one thing for sure. Early was really good at that.

"And yes, it didn't matter who was up there—his mother, his sister, what have you—he wasn't going to give up any part of the plate that he thought belonged to him. But boy, he really did have a good year that year [1959]."

It was better than good. Wynn was the best pitcher in the American League. His record was 22–10, and he pitched a league-leading 255⅔ innings while starting 37 ballgames. When Al Lopez needed a big win in '59, he handed the ball to Gus.

By midseason the rest of the league knew that Wynn was the pitcher of the moment. In a mid-July game, Wynn tossed a two-hit shutout at the Yankees for a 2–0 triumph. The next day the writers were exploring New York manager Casey Stengel's thoughts about the man some called Burly Early.

"He's got everybody in the league scared," Stengel said. "If I had to win one game, I'd hafta say that I'd want him to go. He knows just about all there is to know about pitching."

Wynn had taken an ego bruising the previous two years. There had been clamors for him to retire, suggestions that he could not coax another big winning year out of his right wing. So when Wynn passed the 20-win milestone that summer, he was very pleased. The world knew he could still pitch. He took some convincing himself. It's a sign that the end is near when an athlete begins to question his own mortality. The best players in any sport excel partly through a belief in their own invincibility. If they start to question the very thing that made them great, it is a short hike to retirement.

"I had to prove it," Wynn said, "if only to myself. I knew I could do it. But even I sometimes had my doubts. I suppose a lot of people figured I'd win maybe just 10 or 12 games this year. I had to show myself that I could stay around."

Only a few days before Wynn polished off the Orioles for that 20th victory, he said he was approached by a little old lady—yes, someone older than him—in a hotel lobby, who asked when he was going to quit. It was the question of the hour, and every passerby felt compelled to ask it of Wynn if they even brushed up against him casually.

Wynn answered the little old lady and the sportswriters the same way, especially since he had rekindled his enthusiasm and confidence. "I'll keep going as long as I can," he said. "Maybe I can pitch for three, four more years. If I can't start anymore, maybe I'll relieve. I want to be known as the Old Man of Modern Baseball."

Wynn's field boss, Al Lopez, watched the old warhorse go to the mound every fourth day and bring home win after win for the Sox. Wynn showed him that he could stick around a bit longer.

"I'll bet he's a winning pitcher when he's 42 or 43," Lopez said. "I hope he goes on forever."

Having a pitcher penciled into the rotation for eternity would be a good deal for the White Sox.

Some of Wynn's old Indians buddies marveled at what he was accomplishing. The Indians gave up on Wynn because they thought he was ready to wrap it up. He had been a 20-game winner four times for Cleveland, and no such repeat performances were expected by those residing on the shores of Lake Erie.

(Cleveland) *Plain Dealer* sportswriter Gordon Cobbledick reflected on Wynn's transformation. "Wynn seemed to be living on borrowed time at the end of his Cleveland stay," he wrote, and all evidence supported the notion that "he had had it. But this season, at a time of life when most ballplayers have long since drifted back to the minors, Wynn has been the strong man of the Sox pitching staff, if not, indeed, of American League pitchers."

The best of American League pitchers it was. When the regular season ended, Wynn was voted winner of the circuit's Cy Young Award.

Better with Age

The rest of the American League could not figure out Wynn's resurgence in 1959. Another senior-citizen ballplayer doing that well that season was Enos Slaughter. "Country," as he was nicknamed, was hanging in there with the New York Yankees at age 43.

Casey Stengel revealed that Slaughter's new longevity was attributable to the recently assumed habit of eating sunflower seeds. "Now you tell me—what's Early Wynn's secret? How does he keep going?"

Wynn had a big windup. He raised both hands straight above his head in his stretch, before moving to unleash the pitch. One thing that contributed to Wynn's image as an old man was the little potbelly he had grown that preceded any release. But no, Wynn had not taken up ingesting any foods designed to lead to the fountain of youth. Wynn didn't think there was anything terribly mysterious about his success.

"After all," he said, "I've been pitching a long time. I should know something about throwing that ball."

It was conceded that Wynn's fastball operated more on about four cylinders than the six it used to in his prime, but as pitchers age they grow craftier, relying on more tricks, and Wynn's curveball was

Early Wynn's large windup could still unleash a magnificent fastball even toward the end of his career.

sharper than ever. When pitchers are young studs, and they are full of vim and vigor, they don't hesitate to bring the heat on every throw. When they age, they pick their spots. White Sox catcher Sherm Lollar said Wynn could still jam a hitter with his fastball; he just might set up the slugger differently.

"His breaking stuff is good, but Early gets a lot of strikeouts with his fastball, too," Lollar said, "because he throws it in spots where the batter isn't expecting it."

As the White Sox closed in on the pennant, the city could hardly believe it. Four decades—two full generations—had passed since the team disgraced itself by fixing the 1919 World Series. The Sox had paid their penance, with triple damages. It was pointed out that so much time had gone by that only manager Al Lopez and coaches Ray Berres, Tony Cuccinello, Don Gutteridge, and Johnny Cooney were alive the last time the Sox won the American League title. For all of the joking about Wynn being older than Methuselah, he had actually been born three months after the Black Sox threw the Series.

Winning When Others around You Are Losing

Walter Johnson won 416 games during his major league career but suffered through many bad Washington Senators seasons. How many games might Johnson have won if he had played with the Yankees? No one can know that. Although the Senators did win two pennants when Johnson was nearing the end of his career in the 1920s, they were rarities.

The Senators served time in the second division for years. The phrase "Washington, first in war, first in peace, and last in the American League" was coined for those brutally bad clubs. If people felt sorry for Johnson's exile in Washington, the team was not much better when Wynn played for the Senators between 1939 and 1948, either. When he put together a 17–15 record one season, he earned the type of praise usually reserved for commenting on miracles.

"The fellows all hustle and do the best they can," Wynn told a reporter who questioned the mistakes typically made by others in the Washington lineup. "I have no squawk about my support. Remember, they had a lot to do with the 17 I did win, so why talk about those I didn't?"

Wynn likely would have won many more ballgames if he transferred to the Indians and then on to the White Sox long before he did. If he sounded mellow way back when, he seemed to have less patience as his career was rushing to an end. The young players on the White Sox quaked when they made an error behind Wynn because he would virtually bore holes in them with his laser stare.

There was much less fraternization between teams than there is today when they took the field for batting practice or fielding practice, or when they passed one another on the grass. It was uncommon for the greetings to get too friendly, and Wynn, for one, made it clear that he wanted to be no one's pal. He wanted to scare opposing hitters, not make nice with them. He wanted them shaking when they stepped up to hit.

"No, he didn't make chit-chat with the guys he was going to face," said Turk Lown, another White Sox pitcher of the era. "You didn't see everybody standing around the batting cage laughing and having a good time. Especially not Early. I don't think so. You didn't do that."

Wynn had moments later in his career when he loosened up more, cracked jokes a bit more often, and tried to show that he took himself a little bit less seriously than nuclear science. At the end of his White Sox days, as he was returning to the Indians for his final shot at 300 wins, Wynn said one of his Florida neighbors asked, "Hey, Gus, is it true you played at Cooperstown?" Wynn, telling the story about himself, replied, "Played at Cooperstown? Who the hell do you think invented the game?"

Going After 300

Although the White Sox did not win the World Series, a grateful populace was pretty darned happy about a pennant. Early Wynn was the toast of the town. The joyous experience rejuvenated him, and for the first time he became confident that he could stay in baseball long enough to reach 300 victories.

With 300 always regarded as the benchmark of lasting greatness among hurlers, when Wynn was in the dumps after his first so-so Sox season, he didn't think he could last long enough to join the other 12 (at the time) 300-game winners.

Wynn topped 250 victories in April 1959, and at the time he said making it to 275 was definitely a goal. As for 300, it seemed unlikely, it was out of reach, he admitted. Unless, that is, everything went very well.

But when Wynn posted 22 wins in 1959 he felt it in his bones that he could do it. The old arm had just enough juice left in it. When he turned up for spring training in 1960 after working construction all winter to fine-tune his conditioning, 300 was on his mind.

"I figure two good seasons should put me over the top," Wynn said. "And I'm ready for the first one right now. What has my age got to do with it? Lot of guys in their 20s haven't been winning 20 games lately."

chapter 10

Top of the Mountain and the New-Look White Sox

Ted Kluszewski knocks in one of the five runs he was responsible for in the 1959 World Series.

World Serious

The White Sox had waited 40 years for another crack at a World Series, and they were as hungry as a team could be. In 1959 the Los Angeles Dodgers were playing in their first World Series since relocating to the West Coast, but the Dodgers had finally won a Series for Brooklyn in 1955 before abandoning New York.

It's possible that the World Series has not been played in a more peculiar ballpark, at least not since stadiums were constructed with metal after the dead-ball era. The Los Angeles Coliseum was then, and is now, a football stadium, not a baseball park. It was the Dodgers' temporary home while their new park in Chavez Ravine was being constructed. It was as if a normal ballpark had been supersized by McDonald's. The Coliseum held more than 90,000 fans. They didn't all have good seats, due to the configuration of the diamond instead of a gridiron, but they sure could pack the people in. It was also a ridiculously short poke down the left-field line for a hitter to be rewarded with a home run.

The White Sox had conquered the American League, but even though the Dodgers were not the same old bums from Brooklyn, with some of the big names of the late 1940s and 1950s in retirement, the popularity of some of the old timers made L.A. the favorites. Duke Snider, Gil Hodges, Jim Gilliam, and Carl Furillo still wore Dodger blue, and they were supplemented by hitters like Wally Moon and pitchers like Sandy Koufax (on his way up) and Don Drysdale.

Yet it was the old pro, Early Wynn, who catalogued the win when the Sox decimated the Dodgers, 11–0, in the opener by showing surprising pop in their bats. The hero of the day was Big Klu, who crushed the ball every which way. Ted Kluszewski knocked in five runs with a single and two two-run homers.

Before there was interleague play, there was less empirical knowledge of the champs from the other league. The teams had not played one another during the regular season, and no teams from the home league had played the other circuit's champs. So there were no head-to-head comparisons. Teams had to rely on their scouting staffs to tip off their pitchers about the other team's tendencies.

Wynn went seven innings and gave up just six hits and no runs. He did not attribute it to burning the midnight oil reading scouting reports the night before.

"This World Series scouting business is for the birds," Wynn said. "I'm sure the Dodger scouts told them we were weak hitters. So what happens? We win 11–0. We had reports on how to pitch to the Dodgers, but I paid no attention to them. I had my own scouting system."

Wynn said he studied the wind pattern, but in reality it was probably 20 years of major league pitching experience talking.

Billy Pierce, who had been the team's steadiest starting pitcher during the 1950s, did not draw the nod from manager Al Lopez to start a single game in the Series. He was used in relief, pitching three innings once and merely issuing an intentional walk in another appearance. However, the Game 1 victory that put the Sox up 1–0 in the Series is a game he cites as among the most exciting of his career.

"That first game was 11–0, and with Kluszewski hitting those home runs, we felt we were on our way," Pierce said. "I didn't even play in it. I was in the dugout, and then they sent me to the bullpen to maybe pitch to a left-handed batter. There is some irony in that. But for the White Sox to win the pennant and for us to get to the World Series was great."

Game 1 was the highlight for the White Sox, though. The Dodgers bounced back and captured the Series, four games to two, a series that included a record 92,394 attendance in Game 3. Lopez hated the Coliseum's dimensions because he felt they detracted from the Sox's running game.

"We're a better ballclub anywhere else than we are in the Los Angeles Coliseum," Lopez said in the middle of the Series.

"We are a defensive club with good pitching and speed. The Coliseum robs us of these good points. It isn't the short fence that hurts us because of balls hit against it or over it. Where that short left-field fence handicaps us is that we can't run. You can't go from first to third, and you can't even score from second on a clean hit."

Center fielder Jim Landis took more pride in his fielding than most players in the game. He expected to make all of the routine plays routinely and make the tough plays with only minor difficulty. But he despised the Coliseum.

Landis, like most of the White Sox, played well in the opener, stroking three singles, but that was gravy. He held down his spot in the lineup because of his smoothness with the glove and his ability to cover territory in the outfield. He never felt right in the Coliseum, however.

"It wasn't a ballpark, for God's sake," Landis said years later. "It was a football stadium that they made into a ballfield. It was weird. It wasn't even 300 feet down the left-field line. It took a little more than a pop up to be a home run. You would walk out onto the field and look at it and say, 'What the hell is this? Is this a baseball field?' "

Landis rarely made errors. He had seasonal fielding averages of .995 twice and .993 twice. To him an error was as foreign a term as *sushi* would have been back then.

"You couldn't see with the background," he said. "Hitting and fielding, it was tough to pick up a ball with all of the white shirts. Plus the day games at that time of year, the damned sun was right there. I lost a ball in the sun."

Landis still sounded horrified by the occurrence almost 50 years later.

"People don't realize the ball hit my toes, and it hurt," he said. "It hit my left foot. The ball sort of just kicked off my glove, and luckily, I guess you could say, it went down and hit my toes next."

Trader Bill

For the White Sox, reaching the World Series was a longstanding quest. The town celebrated the pennant with great vigor, but the achievement would have been sweeter if the season culminated in a World Series championship.

Bill Veeck had taken over the ballclub in time for spring training, but it had already been built. The long-term regulars who had starred throughout the 1950s brought home the pennant at last. What was lesser-noticed was a group of very promising young players who were being readied to step in for the aging stars.

The Sox featured Earl Battey as a backup catcher, Johnny Romano as another catcher with promise, Johnny Callison as a promising outfielder, and Barry Latman as an up-and-coming pitcher. All three position players became All-Stars—after being traded away. Veeck and his general manager, the slugging first baseman Hank Greenberg, also traded off hard-hitting Don Mincher and first basemen Norm Cash, who won the American League batting title for the Tigers. Oops.

Veeck didn't want to play the youngsters. He wanted a repeat pennant-winner, counting on the guys who brought it to him the first time. He didn't want to be patient. The moves backfired big time. The White Sox didn't have it in them for another flag run without the infusion of new blood. Wynn couldn't match his Cy Young season. Veeck, usually savvy on player-personnel moves, always savvy about what provided the customer with a rollicking good time, mortgaged the future.

"That was the big mistake he made," pitcher Billy Pierce said of Veeck's wheeling and dealing. "Look at what those players became."

Soon enough, Pierce was gone, too, traded to the San Francisco Giants for the last chapter of his career.

One of the guys who escaped Veeck's housecleaning and stuck around—for another decade—was southpaw Gary Peters. Peters came up to the majors in 1959 and matured into a 20-game winner for the White Sox. He was part of the youth movement that formed a healthy mixture with the veterans, and he benefited from it.

Peters, born in 1937, grew up in Grove City, Pennsylvania. That gave him a conversation starter with another White Sox

Pennsylvania native, Nellie Fox. Sometimes Peters wondered if he didn't have more in common with Fox than Pierce, the second baseman's longtime roommate.

"Billy and Nellie were really great roommates," Peters said. "But Billy didn't drink, and Nellie did. Nellie chewed tobacco and swore. Billy didn't."

Yet they were good roommates.

"Nellie kind of took me under his wing. He was from Pennsylvania, and I was from Pennsylvania. He was a hunter, and I was a hunter. He advised me when I got to the big leagues on salary and stuff like that."

Peters had been up and down between the White Sox and their minor league affiliates, appearing in just a few games per year between 1959 and 1962. Then he had a breakthrough season in 1963, going 19–8.

"When I had that good year in '63, Nellie said, 'Give me a call when you get your contract. Let me know what they offer you.' So I did. It was for like a $2,000 raise. And he said, 'Tear that thing up, put it back in the envelope, and send it back to them.' Hank Greenberg was the general manager. I told Nellie, 'Nah.' He said, 'Do it.'"

An edgy Peters, wondering if he was taking the proper approach, tore up the contract as instructed, put it back in the envelope and sent it back to the White Sox.

"I didn't hear from them," Peters said. "I was Rookie of the Year and won 19 games, but I didn't really think, 'Well, they've got to sign me.' I didn't think that way. I was getting worried. I started to think, 'Gee, maybe they're not going to want me to pitch next year.'

"Finally, Hank Greenberg called me and said, 'I guess you don't want to play next year.' I said, 'Oh, no, I want to play.' So naturally I signed for pretty close to what they originally offered me."

Peters wondered if he might have done better negotiating with owner Bill Veeck, who could make some spontaneously friendly gestures toward players. Veeck occasionally peeled off a $50 bill and told a player who did something special to go buy a new suit.

Manager Eddie Stanky, who replaced Lopez for the 1966 season, did Veeck one better. He institutionalized suits as a reward.

"In his first full year as manager, he liked ground-ball pitchers," Peters recalled. "Tommy John and Joel Horlen and I made batters hit a lot of ground balls. Well, Stanky said, 'Anybody who pitches a complete game and gets 21 ground-ball outs (that's a lot of ground outs), I'll buy you a suit at Spencer's.' That was a good suit place. Between the three of us we got three or four suits in the first half of the season. Stanky cancelled the deal. At the All-Star break he said 'We're not going to do that anymore.'

"He was going broke giving out that many suits."

John, who spent an unlikely 26 years pitching in the majors, especially after having his arm rebuilt by the surgery that came to be named for him, did not sound as if he had the grandest of aspirations in his early White Sox days, which began in 1965, his third major league season.

John finished that season with a 14–7 record and thought that was pretty good.

"Any pitcher up there, except possibly Sandy Koufax, would take a 14–7 record every season and be happy with it," John said. "This would be the best form of security you would have."

Huh?

"If you were to go 14–7 every year in the big leagues," he extrapolated, "you could get a raise and know that you were helping the ballclub." And why not dream of winning 20? "It's when you win 20 games one year and then drop down to 15 or 16 the next that people start saying you had a bad year."

It sounded like the kind of speech someone would have uttered on *M*A*S*H*.

A 1960s Instant Replay

In many ways, while the United States was breaking barriers by forging new directions with civil rights for African Americans and with student protests influencing the conduct of war in Vietnam, the White Sox were reliving the 1950s.

The Sox did not repeat in 1960. Year after year for most of the decade, just as they had in the 1950s before grabbing that pennant, they came close but faltered. Winning records were common; winning it all was out of reach.

It seemed to hurt Al Lopez physically when the White Sox parted with lefty Billy Pierce after the 1961 season.

"I didn't want to do it," he said. "I hated to deal Pierce. He's a wonderful guy and a great pitcher. We've got to give youth a chance to prove its ability. If we kept Billy, we'd have to spot him next year, and we've got too many pitchers now to spot."

By 1964 Jim Landis was the elder statesman of the team in terms of service. Although he wouldn't recognize some of his teammates in a police lineup, he predicted in spring training the Sox could win the pennant. He had other worries, though, besides winning games. In recent seasons Landis's batting average had faded down the stretch. He said he was losing too much weight off his already skinny frame and growing weaker.

"Maybe if I had more weight I'd be more durable," Landis said.

More than 40 years ago steroids were an unknown supplement, and in ballplayer lexicon *steroids* was as strange a word as *Internet*. Landis tried such innovative calorie-pounding methods as drinking three chocolate malteds a day, eating only high-calorie food, and drinking beer liberally. Nothing worked, at least not for long. He gained some weight and lost it again. By the 1964 season Landis had sworn off gimmicks.

"I quit trying to gain weight," he said.

New Slugger on the Block

During the course of their entire existence, the Chicago White Sox were more identified with the knuckleball than the batted ball, better known for fielders cutting off hits headed to the outfield than hitting balls to the outfield themselves.

There were no Babe Ruths or other heavy-duty sluggers wearing Pale Hose during the first half century–plus of the team. Unexpectedly, with the promotion of Bill Melton to the major league roster in 1968, the White Sox found a power hitter who could lose baseballs in the stands and *over* the stands.

In 1968 the new third baseman just kind of felt his way around. By 1969 he was a regular and smacked 23 home runs. In 1970 Melton swatted 33. In 1971, when he banged 33 homers again, he led the American League. No single day, however, compared to the violence his bat wreaked on the ball during a game in June 1969 against the short-lived Seattle Pilots.

The first three times Melton strode to the plate, he belted a home run. Three homers in one game. But the game wasn't over yet. The major league record for homers in a single game is four, tied by many. Melton had the chance to claim a piece of that in the seventh inning. He struck out. Melton came up once more, in the ninth, ripping the ball to deep left field. Instead of clearing the fence, the ball came down fair inside the wall, and Melton raced into second with a double. Three home runs and a double was quite the day's work, and Melton sounded like the most surprised guy in the clubhouse afterward when discussing his authorship of the performance.

"I've never hit three homers in a game anywhere," Melton said. "In fact, I've hit two in a game only twice. And both times it was in the minors."

Even if the crowd thought his last blast might have had the distance to ride over the fence, the contact didn't fool Melton.

"I just didn't get the good meat of the bat on the ball," he said. "It was an inside pitch about letter high, but I caught the ball just about at the end of the label of the bat."

"Auld Lang Syne"

The 1960s were a freeze-frame for White Sox nostalgia. Players made news for every reason except playing. Some died. Some gave up the game. Some retired.

Longtime White Sox pitching mainstay Billy Pierce, who finished his career with the Giants and got the chance to be on another World Series club, retired after the 1964 season.

Ray Schalk compares mitt sizes in 1963, two years before he stepped down from his job at Purdue University. Photo courtesy of AP/Wide World Photos.

"I leave without regret and with only fond memories," he said.

Pierce did a newsman the favor of choosing his personal All-Star, all-opponent team. Although he did see action in the National League for a few years, a quick perusal showed that Pierce was a White Sox–American Leaguer at heart. He named Yogi Berra as catcher; Bill Skowron at first base; Joe Gordon at second; George Kell at third; Phil Rizzuto at short; Ted Williams, Hank Aaron, and Mickey Mantle in the outfield; Bob Feller as a right-handed pitcher; and Whitey Ford as his left-handed pitcher.

There were six Yankees on the private All-Star squad, and Pierce said that he just might have won more than 211 games in his career if he hadn't had to pitch against New York so often.

Nick Altrock died at 88 in early 1965, decades after he ceased playing for the White Sox, but not so long after he had given up clowning at baseball games. Most of that time was spent with the Washington Senators, and between 1921 and 1933 Altrock and fellow Senators coach Al Schacht performed at the World Series. They played ballparks everywhere, making fans laugh, yet for years they did not speak to one another off the diamond.

"We took separate cabs to the theater and separate cabs to get home," Altrock said. "I can't tell you why we didn't speak. I have never told the story. But let's just say we get along better that way."

In early 1965 Ray Schalk, the Hall of Fame catcher who survived the Black Sox Scandal with clean socks, stepped down from his job as assistant baseball coach at Purdue University after 18 years.

"For goodness sake," said Schalk, 72 at the time, "don't say I'm retired from baseball."

He was sensitive to that charge because Schalk was still serving as director of the baseball division of Chicago mayor Richard J. Daley's Youth Foundation. The responsibility included visiting 25 city parks a day in the summer. Chicago's first Mayor Daley was a huge White Sox fan just like his son, current mayor Richard Daley.

Ed Cicotte, the knuckleball artist who was the pivotal bad guy in the Black Sox Scandal for taking $10,000 and demonstrating the fix was in by hitting the first batter with a pitch, died at age 84 on May 5, 1969.

"I admit I did wrong, but I paid for it for the past 45 years," he said a few years before he died, in an interview with Detroit sportswriter Joe Falls. "Sure they asked me about being a crooked ballplayer. But I've become calloused to it. I figure I was crooked in baseball, and they were crooked in something else. I don't know of anyone who ever went through life without making a mistake. Everybody who has ever lived has committed sins of their own.

"I've tried to make up for it by living as clean a life as I could. I'm proud of the way I've lived, and I think my family is, too."

Cicotte spent his waning years as a strawberry farmer in Michigan but said he still received a few letters a week, many from young baseball fans. Some asked about the Black Sox, and he offered advice.

"I tell them I made a mistake and I'm sorry for it," Cicotte said. "I try to tell them not to let anyone push them the wrong way."

The esteemed Luis Aparicio was exiled from the White Sox after the 1962 season in a controversial trade, but he returned to the team closest to his heart for the 1968 season and played three more years in Chicago.

At the start of the 1969 season, Aparicio predicted the Sox would be winners, capturing the Western Division title.

"We're going to surprise a lot of people this year," Aparicio said. "I'm really convinced that we have a better chance to win the division title this year than we had to take the pennant in 1959. You know, nobody thought we'd win back in 1959, not even Bill Veeck, who owned the club."

The skeptics were correct in 1969. The White Sox finished fifth in the west that season. Aparicio did have some highlights, however, collecting his 2,000th career hit at age 35.

"Really, I believe I'm a better player now than I ever was," he said. "Both as a shortstop and a hitter. Maybe I don't make as many spectacular plays, but I know more about how to play the hitters. And another reason I believe I'll be around for a long time is that I don't see anybody who can replace me.

"You know what? Maybe I can play long enough so that my son Luis can take my place!"

chapter 11

Wild Hair and Wild Doings on the South Side

Fans storm the field at Chicago's Comiskey Park on July 12, 1979–Disco Demolition Night–after the first game of a doubleheader against the Detroit Tigers. The promotion by a local radio station turned into a melee after hundreds of disco records were blown up on the field. Photo courtesy of AP/Wide World Photos.

Veeck—as in Back

Glad-handing, fan-friendly owner Bill Veeck gained control of the Chicago White Sox in early 1959, just in time for the team to win its first pennant in 40 years. He tried to improve the roster and failed miserably with a series of bad trades, then despite his hard-fought efforts to establish his ownership, Veeck sold out on doctor's orders and drove off over the horizon to supposed retirement in Maryland in 1961.

Veeck had seemed like a lifer owner, a leader who would retain possession of one of the two Chicago teams in his hometown as long as he lived. But he wasn't willing to pay with his life, so he listened to medical advice to take it easy.

Stunningly, Veeck emerged in 1976 once again as the White Sox owner. Healthier (perhaps), wealthier (possibly), and wiser (he insisted it was so), it was time to roll out the beer-barrel polkas again and treat the fans to the unexpected.

Veeck was never going to be just another millionaire owner in a fancy suit. True to his beliefs, he avoided wearing a tie for any occasion in his second go-around with the Sox, too. But challenging baseball's hidebound ways—from introducing names to the back of uniforms to the exploding scoreboard—Veeck came up with encores that always provoked conversation, even if they sometimes baffled.

Sportshirt always did think out of the box, and when Veeck got to pondering and asking why, he sometimes stepped out onto a dangerous slope. During spring training of 1976 Veeck decided that the old-fashioned flannels, long sleeves, and long pants that had kept players sweating during the hottest months of summer since the game began needed some fine-tuning.

The master of the off-day press conference, Veeck brought baseball writers in one day to view the team's new uniforms. One variety on display, modeled by former outfielder Jim Rivera as part of the team's official uniform selections, included shorts. It was inevitable given the times that the shorts were instantly labeled "hot pants." There was much fast eye-blinking and gaping jaws.

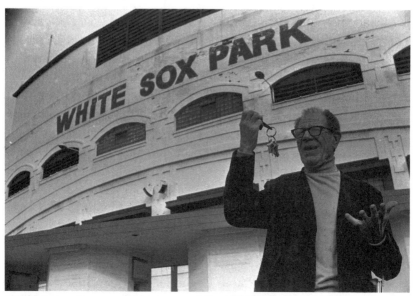

Bill Veeck returns as the owner of the White Sox in 1976. Holding the keys to the park once again, he was heard to say, "It's all mine." Photo courtesy of AP/Wide World Photos.

"Love me!" declared the player known in his active days as Jungle Jim.

Such passion for the outfit was not immediately forthcoming. When asked to describe the new uniforms, Veeck said, "I would use the same description my wife, Mary Frances, used when she saw them: understated elegance."

The scribes were suspicious and wondered if the current players were on board for such a dramatic wardrobe shift. Veeck assured one and all that the Sox would be fine with the idea.

"I'm not worried about the players' reactions," he said. "People are comfortable in shorts today."

He should have been worried. Even Veeck's model didn't seem terribly enthusiastic about using the shorts during a game. Rivera was asked about the prospects of sliding while wearing shorts.

"Hell, no, I wouldn't wear them," he said. "How you gonna slide? They're cool, though, I'll say that."

Standing near Rivera, former Sox pitcher Dan Osinski reached over and pinched Rivera on the knee. Rivera said he did receive a strong reaction from someone of the female species on his way into the press conference. "One girl made fun of me out in the hallway," he said, "and I told her my legs were better looking than hers."

Veeck dismissed the protests emanating from sliding in shorts as long as the players tried it—"hopefully not on their knees."

People may be comfortable taking summer strolls in shorts, wearing them to the beach, or playing basketball, but there was no groundswell of support for the idea of Major League Baseball players wearing shorts. The players hated the shorts, and they almost never wore them.

If the baseball establishment was agog over Veeck's shorts proposal, that was nothing compared to the response when he regained control of the Sox. That was far more surprising. Veeck had been out of the major league limelight for some time, though he had periodically attempted to put together a millionaires' club to buy a team. Everything had fizzled.

Negotiations with the financially hemorrhaging Sox, who were threatening to move to Seattle, went on for months, and while Veeck did not personally have the cash to make a deal on his own, he knew enough moneymen who were interested and willing to pony up. Their commitments, combined with bank loans, allowed Veeck to meet major league financial requirements. It was not as if Veeck was standing outside Marshall Field's with a Salvation Army collection pot, but he invited anyone who had a few shekels in the bank into the ownership group—47 people in all. Initially Veeck's White Sox purchase proposal was turned down by the other major league owners, who were well aware that Veeck had bad-mouthed them repeatedly.

When Veeck, however, showed that he had met every requirement for approval and threatened to go to court to prove it, the owners voted in favor of his acquisition. It was prophecy fulfilled. When Veeck loaded his family into a station wagon and departed Chicago for the wilds of Maryland, one task he devoted himself to was writing his autobiography, *Veeck—As In Wreck*. Typical of

Veeck, he left the door open for a return to baseball with the cryptic commentary: "Sometime, somewhere there will be a ballclub no one really wants. And then ole Will will come wandering along to laugh some more. Look for me under the arc lights, boys. I'll be back."

It took 15 years, but Veeck's words came true when he made his pitch and returned to Chicago as a headliner again. Not incidentally, he saved the storied White Sox from fleeing to a new home in the Pacific Northwest.

Amazingly, short-shorts aside, Veeck was named the 1977 Executive of the Year by *Sporting News*. It was a case where he might have said "I told you so," but he was gracious.

"I'm very flattered," Veeck said. "I realize and appreciate the significance of this award. But in a very real sense, it's unfair. Such an award shouldn't go to an individual. It should go to an entire organization."

By then Veeck had not only made Seattle safe from the White Sox, he had given Sox fans a thrill ride as a sort of American Bicentennial present.

The South-Side Hitmen

Baseball economics had changed dynamically since Veeck sold the Sox in the 1960s. He reacquired the team at a time when Major League Baseball was undergoing seismic shifts. Free agency had taken hold, and the richest teams were making the largest bids for unattached talent.

Veeck had been a public supporter of eradicating baseball's reserve clause, which bound players to teams for life. Now he had to live with the new rules that gave more freedom to players while his team struggled with a smaller bank account than the New York Yankees and others. Veeck knew he needed an infusion of new talent, but he couldn't afford to pay the going rate for high-priced free agents. Instead, he embarked on a rental-player program of sorts.

Pitcher Ken Kravel, a member of the South-Side Hitmen, pitches against the Cleveland Indians on August 29, 1977.

Rather than lock up pricey players with long-term contracts that would sink the franchise, Veeck traded for or signed free agents for one-year deals who would be free to negotiate long-term payoffs with other clubs after the season. In this manner he acquired power hitter Richie Zisk, outfielder Oscar Gamble (he of the mile-high pile of hair), and third baseman Eric Soderholm.

There were no expectations that the White Sox of 1977 would be contenders in the American League. But under the savvy touch of manager Bob Lemon, the mix of old and new guys blended to make a serious run at the pennant. The Sox held down first place in the American League West for six weeks starting July 1 and finished with 90 victories while driving Chicago fans into a delirium.

It was far from a perfectly made-up team, but one thing the White Sox possessed was power in the middle of the lineup. A home run got the Comiskey Park crowds salivating and demanding curtain calls from their unexpected heroes. Gamble hit 31 home runs and batted .297. Zisk hit 30 home runs and drove in 101 runs. Soderholm hit 25 homers. And such accomplished hitters as Ralph Garr (a one-time National League batting champion), Chet Lemon, and Lamar Johnson always took good cuts.

Although fans loved to watch Gamble hit, they marveled at his ability to keep his baseball cap on his head over his mushrooming Afro. At a time when $33 seemed more appropriate for a ransom note, Gamble admitted paying that much for a haircut. People wondered what the barber did. Of course, the major trimming occurred when Gamble played for the Yankees, under team orders. When he joined the Sox, Gamble let it all grow back.

There was never any pretense that Gamble or Zisk would be around for more than a season unless they fell in love with Chicago and were willing to forego hundreds of thousands of dollars in the free-agent market. Zisk, a National League product who came over from the Pirates, said he was glad to be somewhere his home-run hitting prowess was appreciated and said he wanted to make the exploding scoreboard work for him.

"I can't wait to set the thing off," Zisk said before his successful Sox season.

Zisk set off his share of fireworks—almost as many as were sent skyward for July 4 celebrations.

Soderholm was happier than either of the others to be in Chicago. He had been a steady player for the Twins but missed all of 1976 with a severe left-knee injury, and some doctors suggested he would never play again. Soderholm was just grateful Veeck signed him, and when his stroke returned to ease his mind, he realized he liked being in Chicago. Soderholm won the Sporting News Comeback Player of the Year Award for the American League.

"It's been a fantastic year," said Soderholm, who also batted .280 and drove in 67 runs and spoke favorably of his feelings for Veeck. "Bill and I were both in the depths of despair at this time last year, but we had great years. Bill was going broke, and I didn't know if I still had a career. But we both made it."

Somewhat overshadowed that season by the big guns was a young player named Chet Lemon, who was about to blossom into an All-Star. Lemon made his mark in the sport both with the White

Sox and the Detroit Tigers. The Sox acquired Lemon from the Oakland A's when he was just 20.

Larry Doby, the first African American player in the American League when he was brought to the majors in 1947 by Veeck, then owner of the Indians, was the White Sox hitting coach and gave special attention to Lemon. The young player also studied Zisk and Gamble.

"Having guys like Zisk and Gamble in the lineup helped take some pressure off me for sure," Lemon said.

He hit 19 home runs and batted .273 in 1977. Headline writers in future years liked to point out that for A's owner Charlie Finley the trade "was a Lemon." The South-Side Hitmen season was near the beginning of a 16-year career for Lemon that included three All-Star selections.

The fans adopted—and nicknamed—the South-Side Hitmen of 1977. They chanted, offered spontaneous standing ovations, and dreamed of miracles. And the team set a then–single-season attendance record of 1,657,135.

It was a special year in White Sox history. When the season ended, Zisk was a free agent. Veeck tried to keep him, but he couldn't compete with other teams' offers, and Zisk moved on to the Texas Rangers. Gamble left for the San Diego Padres.

Knowing he would always be playing catch-up, Veeck sought to rebuild by taking on fresh players who would also test the free-agent market, but never again did the package come together so smoothly or produce as much excitement as the South-Side Hitmen did for one glorious summer.

A Slugger Emerges

From the "Hitless Wonders" to the "Go-Go White Sox," the Chicago American League franchise had never been noted for its power hitting. Babe Ruth could have hit one-against-nine and defeated the Sox in a home-run derby. The White Sox never had a player lead the league in homers.

Then out of nowhere came Bill Melton. As the decade changed from the 1960s to the 1970s, Melton entrenched himself as the new White Sox third baseman, and in 1971 (albeit with a small number by current standards) Melton led the American League in homers with 33.

Melton was meltin' the fastballs from opposing pitchers on the final weekend of the season, smashing three homers to win the crown by one blast over Reggie Jackson and Norm Cash. As the season wound down, manager Chuck Tanner said that there would be no champagne in his clubhouse without a first-place finish. For third place, where the Sox finished, the reward would only be beer and chicken. However, the team changed its mind when Melton led the league, and the bubbly was poured to honor him.

Actually, about as much champagne was poured over Melton as into his mouth. His entire body was sopping wet in the locker room once the achievement went into the books.

"It smells funny, but it feels great," said Melton, who apparently did not frequent the fanciest restaurants on New Year's Eve or other special occasions.

When a young player emerges with a milestone accomplishment it is usually described as a herald of something big. But Melton ran into bad luck the next year with a bad back, stemming from a herniated disk, that almost ruined his career. His 1972 season was a write-off, but he returned in 1973 with a solid 20-homer, 87-RBI year. His return was a vote of confidence for an experimental treatment called chemonucleolysis, which involves injections of an enzyme that comes from the leaves of the papaya plant.

For two years out of three Melton was a walking miracle, first hitting all those home runs, and then making a comeback through the medical treatment of the year.

Fluttering to Success

The entries in *The Baseball Encyclopedia* are arranged in alphabetical order, but if they were listed in chronological order everyone would think Wilbur Wood's page was in the wrong spot.

Knuckleballer Wilbur Wood, pitching here in 1974, was the steadiest and most successful White Sox pitcher in the 1970s.

Wood was the steadiest and most successful White Sox pitcher of the 1970s, posting statistics that seemed to be from another era and that seem only more formidable and unreal with the passage of time. Wood's pitching line more resembles one of the hurler's from the dead-ball era rather than the modern era.

For four straight years, 1971–1974, Wood won at least 20 games. However, he lost no fewer than 13 games, and in 1973 he lost 20. For five straight years (including 1975) Wood started no fewer than 42 games with a high of 49 in 1972 and 1973. For four straight years between 1971 and 1974, Wood threw no less than 320 innings. In 1972 he pitched 376⅔ innings, the most by any pitcher dating back to the 1920s.

Wood was not only a man out of time, he was a man for all time. His left arm never hurt, he sometimes started on two days' rest, and begged his managers to let him start both games of a doubleheader. What gave Wood a flexibility that almost no other pitcher in the history of baseball possessed was a flummoxing knuckleball that left no wear and tear on his left arm.

"Everybody thinks I should be more tired, but I'm not," Wood said during the 1971 season. "I feel no difference, physically or mentally, between two and three days of rest. Sometimes I don't even know myself how much rest I've had. A lot of guys could do it. They just don't realize it."

Wood is from Massachusetts, and he grew up in the Red Sox chain. He was a more traditional fastball-curveball pitcher during early struggles with the Red Sox and Pittsburgh Pirates. When the Pirates cut him, Wood realized he needed another pitch if he was going to get another chance to play in the majors. He worked hard on his knuckler and then wound up with the White Sox in 1967.

At the time, Hoyt Wilhelm, perhaps the greatest knuckleball artist of all time and the first relief pitcher elected to the Hall of Fame, was on the team. It set up a perfect mentor-student situation for Wood. Wilhelm, who lasted in the majors until he was 50 years old, was living proof that the knuckleball was ignorant of age.

For a while it seemed as if Wilhelm could keep collecting a major league paycheck until after he requested his major league pension. When he was 48, and a dozen members of the White Sox roster had not even been born when he made his professional debut in the minors, Wilhelm said he was sick of being asked when he was going to retire.

"Everybody keeps asking whether I'm about ready to hang them up," Wilhelm said. "But that hasn't even entered my mind. The way I feel I don't know why I shouldn't go on for a few more years. My legs are strong, and my arm feels good. So why quit?"

When someone was trying to verify Wilhelm's age he said he was "33 going on 40," neither of which was correct. Leo Durocher turned Wilhelm into a reliever when he played for the New York Giants, and the combination of coming out of the bullpen and throwing the knuckler kept his arm young, he said.

However, Wood become a White Sox starter—his first love— after Wilhelm gave him pointers to develop his knuckler. He was making 76 or 77 appearances a year for Chicago, but the Sox needed help in the rotation. The guy who couldn't make the cut to stay on a major league roster only a few years earlier was a 20-game winner by 1971.

"I've thrown a knuckleball almost as long as I've been pitching," Wood said. "I started fooling around with it while I was still in high school. However, it's never been more than just an extra pitch I'd toss in once in a while just to get the batter off stride a little. But since talking to Wilhelm, it's become my main pitch. And I've certainly had good luck with it."

Wood praised Wilhelm heavily for his generosity with advice and said the older pitcher "sold me" on the knuckler as his number one pitch, while also providing some secret tips. Soon enough Wood was being called "the knuckleball wizard" by *Sporting News* and incurred the wrath of batters who looked foolish when they swung wildly at the ball fluttering past them at perhaps 70 mph.

Making it even worse for the hitters who strode to the plate with determination furrowing their brows and a glint of anger in their eyes was that Wood weighed more than 200 pounds, easily, and it was not spread equally over his six-foot frame. Rather, it was concentrated in his stomach, earning him such unflattering descriptions as "beer belly" or "porky."

One player teased Wood by saying that he could pass for a beer vendor at the park if he went to pick up a selling tray. Wood said none of the comments bugged him.

"I need all that weight in the middle to keep my balance," he said.

Wood didn't care if the players were laughing at him, as he possessed the generosity of the soul to laugh with them. Of course, given that he was selected for three American League All-Star teams, Wood also had the *last* laugh.

It only seemed as if the White Sox had cornered the market on knuckleballers, but at various times during the decade, the team took possession of another mighty fine thrower who, unfortunately for Chicago, had most of his best years elsewhere.

Southpaw Jim Kaat played just 2½ of his 25 major league seasons with the Sox, but the years between 1973 and 1975 might have been the most important of his career. Some thought

Kaat was finished after he came over from the Minnesota Twins, but he adopted a new pitching motion, rapidly speeding up his delivery, and he won 20 games in a season twice for the Sox.

"It's not Jim Kaat," Sox manager Chuck Tanner said. "It's a new guy with the same name. They're two different people."

Kaat's new quick-release was derided by opposing managers as a "quick pitch." They pleaded that it was against the rules, but the umps ruled in Kaat's favor. Pitching coach Johnny Sain, whom many consider the greatest of all at tutoring hurlers, was instrumental in developing Kaat's adopted speed-up style. Sain said that aging pitchers sometimes must adapt to circumstances. For his part, Kaat said he couldn't be bothered worrying about the umpires every time he reared back to throw.

"Shucks, I can't be watching the umpire all night," he said.

So Kaat threw, the pitches counted, and he ended up playing another 10 seasons after joining the Sox.

Disco Demolition Fame and Flames

Bill Veeck was an idea man, a genius of promotion with the common touch. He learned from his father, William, who was president of the Chicago Cubs when young Bill was growing up. And he taught his own son, Mike, well. Mike Veeck worked in the front office as promotions director with his dad during Bill Veeck's ownership stint.

To prove he had not lost his touch, on April 9, 1976, starting his second ownership tenure with the Sox, Bill Veeck, business manager Rudie Schaffer, and manager Paul Richards dressed as the threesome emblematic of the Spirit of '76, complete with fife and drum.

It was a splendid stunt that left them laughing in the aisles of Comiskey Park, the way Bill Veeck always liked it. Alas, Veeck's most infamous idea turned unexpectedly sour and unfortunately tainted his son Mike's career when Disco Demoltion Night on July 12, 1979, went awry.

Heavily promoted by popular Chicago deejay Steve Dahl as a counterpoint to the disco craze sweeping the nation, the plan, first and foremost, was to fill the ballpark. That part worked fine. More than 47,000 people showed up for a White Sox doubleheader against the Detroit Tigers—on a Thursday night. Anyone who brought a disco music album to the park was admitted for 98¢. Part of the night's appeal for disco-haters was that between games of the doubleheader, Dahl would destroy those records with fireworks. The big-bang theory.

Dahl, who is still a well-known radio personality in Chicago, was fired from his job when his radio station went to an all-disco format. While many saw that as a badge of courage worthy of appreciation in the music wars, Veeck offered Dahl the opportunity to gain a measure of revenge on the entire music form. Even Dahl said he was shocked at how well his campaign drummed up antidisco sentiment.

The park was full to overflowing, with thousands gathered outside clutching their disposable disco records. The Tigers won the first game, 4–1, and then came the main event. As scheduled, Dahl blew up a crate of disco records. However, fans were so riled up, so stoked, that they began rushing onto the field. Easily over-powering the limited security presence, the mob's unleashed fury soon wreaked havoc on more than the vinyl. Fans knocked over a batting cage, burned signs, and ripped up the field, creating huge, pothole-sized gouges. Records flew through the air like flying saucers as the fans rampaged. The mini-riot against disco resulted in 37 arrests and a ruined baseball field. Mike Veeck later said so many of the young people were stoned that the event was too peaceful to be termed a riot.

That season, before he moved on to the Cubs, broadcaster Harry Caray was working for the White Sox. Similar to the method of playing "The Star-Spangled Banner" to bring grouchy masses to attention during past trying situations, Caray sought to defuse tension by singing "Take Me Out to the Ballgame." It didn't work.

Bill Veeck was out on the field with a microphone pleading, "Will you please return to your seats?" That didn't work, either.

Former Cubs star Don Kessinger had moved crosstown and was a player-manager for the White Sox. Sensing the menace in the air, he wanted no part of sending his team onto the field for game number two.

"It was just such an unbelievable deal," he recalled in 2006. "I just wanted to make sure that night that we got all of the players out of the dugout and into the locker room between games. I had the door locked so nobody could get in or out. I think it was one of those promotions that was too successful. It was just a different night because at least half the fans were there for something other than a baseball game."

The second game was called off, and the White Sox were ordered to forfeit to the Tigers. It cost Bill Veeck $75,000 to repair the field. This was particularly stinging for Veeck, whose promotions always had a dual purpose—making the fans happy and making money. This scheme made the fans mad and lost money. Not what he was after.

In a 2004 *Chicago Tribune* interview, Mike Veeck, now part owner of eight minor league baseball teams after helping put fans in the seats for other major league teams, said the disco protest kind of took the place of previous mass gatherings.

"This was almost 10 years after Woodstock," Mike Veeck said. "People didn't have much to throw themselves into. Disco bashing became a cause simply because there was nothing else around."

Later Mike Veeck coauthored a book about his life titled *Fun Is Good*. In it he wrote that his ability to handle and overcome adversity is one of his strengths, and he highlighted (or lowlighted) his hand in Disco Demoltion Night as a key example.

"For years," he said, "I looked at Disco Demolition as the end of my life. I had a chance, and I blew it."

As front man for the team, Bill Veeck took much of the heat in the fallout of national coverage. But Disco Demolition Night was really Mike Veeck's baby. It was not, however, by any means the end of his life or the end of his professional baseball involvement. And the sport has been better for it wherever he has traveled.

chapter 12

Characters

Dick Allen played for the Sox from only 1972 to 1974, but he was the highest-paid player in Major League Baseball at that time.

Richie Allen or Dick Allen?

Philadelphia Phillies fans were annoyed by Richie Allen. Chicago White Sox fans revered Dick Allen.

The man of two names was a terrific baseball player in both cities, but he was viewed as a disruptive troublemaker in one (with clubhouse confrontations and missed airplane flights on his résumé) and as the key man on the club in the other. No one will ever know for sure, but Allen claimed race was the issue in his being "misunderstood" in Philadelphia, but he felt warmly received in Chicago.

It is always important to place Allen in the context of his times—the late 1960s and early 1970s—when Americans were just absorbing the concept of civil rights for all. Allen wore an Afro haircut, and his wife, Barbara, was once involved in a car chase, pursued by four men displaying a Confederate flag. That would give anyone a chip on their shoulder.

Whatever swirled around him, Allen ignored it well enough to emerge as a massively productive hitter in both places. Allen spent only 1972, 1973, and 1974 of his 15-year major league career with the White Sox, but they were among his finest years, and he probably should have stuck around longer.

Regardless of whether he was slamming the ball over the outfield fence or making outspoken comments, Allen was a magnet for the media. He posed for the cover of the June 17, 1972, issue of *Sports Illustrated* while juggling three baseballs and with a cigarette dangling from his lips. It was a classic photo and was accompanied by a headline reading "Chicago's Dick Allen Juggles His Image."

In 1972 Allen stroked a league-leading 37 home runs and 113 RBIs while batting .308 and won the American League Most Valuable Player Award in a landslide vote. When the announcement was made, Allen said he was surprised, that he thought Oakland's Joe Rudi would win the trophy.

"I hope I'm worthy of this honor," Allen said.

Two seasons later he hit 32 homers for Chicago. Allen's biggest fan in Chicago was manager Chuck Tanner, which probably helped. Tanner knew Allen when he was growing up in Wampum, Pennsylvania, the state that both men called home. Allen disliked being called Richie, but he couldn't shake it until Tanner, aware of his feelings, began calling him Dick.

Tanner, regarded as a players' manager, uttered the most memorable baseball quote of his career when asked about how he would "handle" the arrival of Allen in his clubhouse.

"People said you can't handle Allen," Tanner said. "Well, you 'handle' animals. You communicate with people."

Years later, Tanner remains in touch with Allen, who raises horses in Pennsylvania, and praises him unreservedly.

"He was the guy who carried us on his back," Tanner said in 2007. "He had the greatest individual year of any player I ever managed, ever, in almost 19 years. I didn't care what they said [in the National League]."

Allen grew up in poverty, one of nine children supported by their mother, Era, part Cherokee, and with older brothers oriented toward athletics. One of them played against Chuck Tanner as a high schooler. In 1963 Allen was the first African American player for the Arkansas Travelers of Little Rock in the International League, and, despite applause from the majority, faced "Nigger Go Home" signs and inflammatory phone calls from some bigots.

After Allen blasted a 470-foot home run to Old Comiskey Park's center field to help win a game against the Yankees, Tanner gushed, "He's Babe Ruth, Rogers Hornsby, and Ty Cobb all put together."

As he talked to the media on the day of the August 1972 swat, Allen peeled off his uniform to reveal that he was superstitious. His underwear had several holes, and Allen said he couldn't change them during a Sox hot streak. Perhaps picturing a Jack Nicklaus–caliber driver, a reporter asked Allen why he didn't play golf.

"I like to hit the ball and have somebody else chase it," Allen replied.

To illustrate how times have changed, at the time Allen signed a three-year deal to play for the White Sox, he was the highest-paid player in baseball at either $675,000 or $750,000, depending on the accuracy of reports at the time. (Hank Aaron had been the previously highest-paid with a $600,000, three-year contract.) That was total, not per season for Allen. It was noted in some newspapers that although president Richard Nixon was paid a $200,000-a-year salary, he also had a broader, well-rounded expense account that made him better-compensated than Allen. The first $1 million-a-year ballplayer still lay in the future, but it's been quite some time since presidents made as much money as professional athletes.

Although fans sometimes forget their history, Allen was one of the best and most prominent players in the game during his prime. But even during his season of greatest achievement in Chicago Allen was too much of a hot-button personality to attract sponsor endorsements.

"No, never in my life have I been asked to do commercials," Allen said in 1973. "I can't complain. You know, I had a bad reputation before I got to Chicago. I don't blame anybody. Maybe it's me. Maybe it's because I'm black. You know, that could have something to do with it."

Allen surprised Tanner and his teammates when, just two weeks before the end of the 1974 season, he announced his retirement from baseball at the age of 32.

"This is hard for me to say. I've never been happier anywhere than here. It's tough to walk away from the game I've been playing since I was this high," Allen said while holding his hands at waist level on his 5'11", 190-pound frame.

At the time, reporters suspected that Allen's motivation was frustration over continuing shoulder and back injuries, which he refused to use as an excuse. However, always enigmatic, Allen made an abrupt turnaround in the off season and resurfaced with the Phillies again for the 1975 season, one of his final three seasons. None were as productive as his time spent with the White Sox.

A Corker

Albert Belle always seemed one step away from a raging fit. He glared with the best of them when scorned reporters approached his locker. He snarled at fans that had the temerity to ask for autographs. He threw a ball into the stands in anger. He tried changing his name from Joey to Albert, but little changed with it. Finally, Belle was exposed by baseball authorities for using a corked bat in play.

On July 15, 1994, Belle, who established his slugging reputation in Cleveland, was still a member of the Indians. The Indians were playing against the White Sox at Comiskey Park, and Sox manager Gene Lamont asked umpire Dave Phillips to investigate Belle's bat. Phillips could not initially tell that anything was amiss with the bat, but he removed it from the game and placed it in his locker in the bowels of the stadium. Play continued.

Apparently it was no secret to at least certain Indians that Belle was using an illegal bat. Teammate Jason Grimsley, who came clean about his role five years later, wiggled through a crawl space and slithered into the umps' changing room. He replaced the confiscated corked bat in an attempt to protect Belle.

Belle hit 36 home runs that season and 52 the next year. When he became a free agent, the White Sox signed him to a five-year, $55-million contract for the 1997 season.

"They didn't have to wine me and dine me or take me to a Bulls game," Belle said. "Once I heard about what they were offering and their commitment to winning, and that my opinion was valued about what could make us a better team, I was sold on them."

During the negotiation process, Belle said he never once thought about the Sox being the team that blew the whistle on him and the corked bat.

"My standard line on that is going to be that I had amnesia and that I can't remember what happened," Belle said. "Actually, the way I look at it is that, at the time, the White Sox were trying to do anything to dethrone us as champions. But it backfired. All it did was piss us off and help us grow together as a team and become better."

It was the right time to get out of Cleveland, Belle felt, and Chicago seemed like a welcoming town. He even complimented the media.

"Chicago is a great place to make a fresh start and knows how to embrace stars," he said. Unlike Cleveland. I'm talking about the media, mainly." A bouquet thrown to Chicago scribes?

Briefly, Belle seemed relaxed in his new environment and signed more autographs than he had in the past. He hit 30 homers for Chicago that year and a team-record 49 in 1998 before disembarking for the Baltimore Orioles. Belle's career ended suddenly in 2000 because of a degenerating hip.

Orta Just What Was Ordered

Probably not a fan in Comiskey Park knew the name Jorge Orta before the young Mexican infielder made his White Sox debut at the age of 21 in 1972. They liked what they saw right away, though.

No one was more serious about making himself into a solid hitter and about improvement than Orta, who hailed from Mazatlan. He probably never would have been happy with his batting stroke unless he hit 1.000, like Chip Hilton of boys' baseball fiction. Orta's father, Pedro, was a renowned player considered comparable in skill to Minnie Minoso. However, Pedro chose not to try to cross the color barrier and established a respected career in Mexico instead of the United States.

The younger Orta was inserted as the Sox shortstop for 18 games as a rookie even though he had not played the position. He had a shortage of experience with another facet of daily life, as well. Orta did not speak English beyond being able to say hello. Orta worked on the baseball end, and teammates helped with his language skills. After a few weeks in the big time, Orta knew how to order a steak, and he knew what the word *pennant* meant in English as well as Spanish.

General manager Roland Hemond, who had friends in the Mexican League, acted on a tip about Orta and signed him late the season before and then sent Orta to the Florida Instructional League in the fall. So he was less of a surprise to management tracking his future than to fans.

During his early years in the majors, even as he shifted to other infield positions, Orta seemed almost scared to smile. He was described more often than not as scowling, but not at his circumstances in the big leagues. Rather because of his alleged shortcomings as a hitter.

"I'm not a good hitter right now," he told a reporter. He was batting .315. You'd hate to see his slump when it was coming around the bend.

When Orta was going through the most challenging adjustment period in the majors, on the way to a 16-year career, he was tutored by none other than Dick Allen. Manager Chuck Tanner said Orta even copied Allen's "mannerisms at the plate." Orta was never the power hitter Allen was, but there were worse role models for someone who wanted to talk hitting.

"He always tries to talk to me," Orta said of Allen in 1974. "He likes to teach young ballplayers."

Orta finished the 1974 season with a .316 average, the best of his career.

And although he never formally acted as a coach with a major league team, Allen satisfied Tanner's faith in him as a valuable resource for up-and-coming players.

Double-Duty DeBusschere

Making it to the roster of any professional sports team defies the odds. Teenagers may excel at all sports when they are in high school, but they are forever being advised to choose one and specialize in it. They will never make it to the top of any sport if they spread their talents too thin, they are told.

The scholastic three-sport athlete has almost vanished. Still, some rare athletes prove they have what it takes to make a mark in two sports. In the case of 1960s White Sox pitcher Dave DeBusschere, it turned out he was good enough to make the team while he played for the Detroit Pistons of the NBA, but that his true sport was basketball.

DeBusschere suited up for the Sox in the 1962 and 1963 seasons. His 3–4 record the second year represents his only decisions. Later DeBusschere starred for the New York Knicks championship teams and was an esteemed basketball executive before dying young of a heart attack in 2003.

When he was 22 and still trying to make the White Sox roster after earning a job with the Pistons, DeBusschere described playing both sports as "breakfast and dinner. They're two different meals, but they both taste good. It depends when you eat them. I like baseball in the summer and basketball in the winter."

DeBusschere had a contemporary role model to follow in trying to make it big in both sports. Gene Conley won a World Series ring pitching for the Milwaukee Braves in 1957 and more than one world title ring playing in the front court for the Boston Celtics in the 1950s and 1960s.

"He tells me it's not as tough to combine the sports as everyone says," DeBusschere said. "I've got to agree with Gene in one respect. People say it can't be done. Yet they don't have to do it. Gene does, and it hasn't hurt him."

Conley got more grief from his baseball teams than he ever did from the Celtics when missing games or spring training. DeBusschere gave up trying to combine the sports after two seasons and continued on to a full-time NBA career. Statistically he was a better basketball player than baseball player, so he probably made the right choice.

Everything Ventured, Everything Gained

Robin Ventura was one of the greatest college baseball players of all time. College baseball never gets the attention of college football and basketball, so some amazing careers go unmentioned. In three seasons at Oklahoma State, Ventura batted .428 with 68

Robin Ventura, one of the best third basemen in White Sox history, hits against the Oakland A's on May 18, 1998.

home runs and 308 RBIs in 210 games. He recorded a 58-game hitting streak. That's two more games than Joe DiMaggio's major league mark. Enough said.

Ventura, one of the best third baseman in White Sox history, broke in with Chicago in 1989 and spent the majority of his 16-year major league career with the club. He was an All-Star in 1992 with a career-high of 34 home runs and 105 RBIs in 1996, and he won six career Gold Gloves. And almost from his first minutes in Chicago Ventura volunteered his time visiting sick kids at Chicago Children's Memorial Hospital.

"A friend of mine was interning there, and he would just call me up, and I would go over there on my own and see some kids without taking the TV cameras that come with the White Sox," Ventura said. "It's a little easier to talk to kids when you're not with a bunch of cameras."

Ventura hit 294 career home runs—good, but not phenomenal, in an era that emphasized slugging. But Ventura carved out an intriguing niche by turning into Superman when striding to the plate with the bases loaded. During his career Ventura walloped 18 grand slams, tied with Willie McCovey behind Lou Gehrig, Manny Ramirez, and Eddie Murray for the most bases-clearing homers—all five hit many more homers overall. He just possessed a talent for smacking grand slams, and in 1999 he became the first major league player to hit grand slams in both games of a doubleheader for the Mets, his team of the moment. After the game Ventura turned off his phone and missed congratulatory calls from relatives all over the nation and didn't bother to celebrate with any parties.

"A neighbor said, 'Hey, good night,'" Ventura said. "That was about it."

No big deal. Yes, it can easily be concluded that eight RBIs on two hits is a good night. Ventura was hard to impress when it came to grand slams. After all, he hit two in a game for the White Sox in 1995. Maybe his blasé approach was for the best.

"The times you try to do it, you hit it 10 feet," Ventura said. "My personal history has been like that. If I ever go up trying, I can't do it."

For years Ventura was a White Sox leader in the field and at bat. He was a staple in the lineup, who six times played at least 150 games per season. When Ventura got hurt, though, he really got hurt. In spring training of 1997, Ventura broke his right leg in two places and dislocated his ankle while sliding into home plate.

The gruesome accident, and the pain evidenced on Ventura's face and through his moans, made three fans pass out and teammate Ozzie Guillen cover his own face with a towel so he wouldn't have to see the hurt in Ventura's eyes. Instantly, coach Joe Nossek wondered if it was a career-ending injury.

"When it happened, it was like somebody shot the team," catcher Rick Wrona said.

Or shot Ventura like an injured racehorse on the track.

Ventura sweated and strained and made himself healthy. When he returned to play 54 games for Chicago that season, beginning on July 24, he wasn't even limping. He spent six weeks in a cast, 10 more weeks rehabbing, then a week swinging at minor league pitching. Ventura then turned in another full-time, 161-game season in 1998 before wrapping up his career with the Mets, Yankees, and Dodgers by 2004.

Ventura was a popular clubhouse guy with the White Sox during his career, though his humor and pranks were more subtle, behind-the-scenes jokes than loud, stand-up comedy routines. During the 1995 season, outfielder Mike Cameron returned to his locker one day only to learn that the outfit he wore to the park was no longer present and accounted for. No one made any type of claim, but if Cameron wanted to step out of the ballpark wearing anything besides a towel, he was going to have to wear a pair of paisley bellbottoms and a suede coat that was too small and tight all around. Cameron could only hope that no photographers from GQ lurked in the side streets outside the park. Ventura was the one responsible for the clothing switch.

On another occasion, when longtime White Sox trainer Herm Schneider was out of commission, Ventura dressed up as the trainer and carried around tape and scissors. No one noted if Ventura cured any previously resistant diseases.

After four hours of surgery for his grisly injury, he truly wondered for a short time if he would play again. But Schneider reassured him. Not only would Ventura play again, he would play again that season. Schneider was right.

When Ventura was healed well enough to play—and play at full strength and full speed—it was Schneider who worried that the player would be injured again on a fluke play. He disliked watching Ventura run around the bases and take slides that were once quite normal for him.

"He has no fear," Schneider said. "I was scared to death."

Late in Ventura's career, when he was playing with the Los Angeles Dodgers, Ventura added one more skill to his repertoire. During a June game, when they were trailing 13–0 to the Angels in the eighth inning, the Dodgers put Ventura into the game as a relief pitcher. Ventura threw 12 pitches for his three outs, surrendering one single. His fastball traveled at the speed of a knuckleball at 72 mph.

Emerging unscathed meant that Ventura claimed a 0.00 earned-run average. He was also content to retire with that number next to his name and swore off pitching again.

"I was not very good," he said. "I can honestly say that."

The Dodgers made it to the 2004 playoffs, and after they were eliminated by the St. Louis Cardinals, Ventura announced his retirement in the locker room. Reduced to the role of a utility player, he said he knew it was time to go. One of the main reasons he cited for retiring was the steady deterioration of his ankle. Despite the successful comeback, the ankle hurt in that spring-training slide continued to haunt him.

"I knew my ankle was getting progressively worse each year," Ventura said. "I knew it wouldn't be fair to come back here...and not be able to be more than just a pinch-hitter."

Far away, the *Chicago Tribune* took note of Ventura's departure from the game, writing that "Ventura was perhaps the lowest-keyed, highest-production player in modern history. You see, he had that inner fierce fire, it was just covered with an outward 'aw, gee' shrug."

Ventura's old teammates and buddies—manager Ozzie Guillen and coaches Greg Walker, Joey Cora, and Harold Baines—were running the White Sox on the field, and it seemed natural for him to join up if an opening came up. Not right away, Ventura said. He wanted to spend time with his family. And he has stayed away from full-time coaching. But he has never removed his connection to the White Sox from his mind.

"I will always feel like I am a White Sox," Ventura said.

chapter 13
Bright Spots Shy of Glory

Despite never fully recovering after his surgery, Bo Jackson proved to be a real asset for the Sox in the early 1990s.

The Best There Is—for a Year

White Sox fans flash serene, beatific looks on their faces when anyone mentions the 1983 season. The team made memories, and no one is more connected to or symbolizes that division-winning team more than pitcher LaMarr Hoyt. Hoyt won 24 games and the Cy Young Award in the American League that season.

He was at the top of his game, and the White Sox were at the top of the West Division. They won 99 games and took the division by an astounding 20 games. Hoyt was a pivotal player in that run. Few realize, however, how close Hoyt came to giving up the sport before he ever hit the majors.

Hoyt was in the New York Yankees organization but was traded to the White Sox in 1977.

"I had fallen out of grace with the management of the White Sox," Hoyt said, "and I had fallen from AAA to A. I played in Appleton, Wisconsin, in 1978 and ended up winning 20 games that season. They wanted to send me to the Fall Instructional League in Florida, and I go, 'Wait a minute. What are you people doing? You keep sending me backwards. I'm 22 years old. I've been playing professional baseball four seasons. I've played winter ball in Venezuela. I'm a little more experienced than just A-ball.' So I quit and went home to South Carolina."

Hoyt felt his talent was being disrespected and was going to try a new career in South Carolina. He was back in the south for a week or more when the White Sox talked him into returning to Appleton.

"So I went, but my whole argument was I've gone there and won 20 games, so what else do you expect me to do?" Hoyt said. "I was told they wanted me to get back to the same level I had showed in the Yankees organization. I said, 'Whatever it takes.'" When Hoyt went back to Appleton he had a heart-to-heart talk with general manager David Hirsch, and the message he picked up was simple: This was his last stop, his last chance, and he had to kick it into high gear and make a splash.

"What he told me probably turned my attitude around totally because he told me matter-of-factly, like, 'This is it, son. You need to have the year that they expect, and you need to throw the ball the way they expect you to throw it.'"

At the end of the season the White Sox again asked Hoyt to play some fall baseball in Florida. He went to Sarasota, and Tony LaRussa, in the early stages of minor league managing in what will surely become a Hall of Fame managing career, monitored Hoyt's work.

"That's when I first met Tony," Hoyt said. "He would come out and watch me throw because he needed help for his team. He'd known my experience and that I wasn't just an ordinary A-ball pitcher to look at."

Hoyt was throwing hard and accurately, as well as he ever had in his life, with LaRussa standing just three feet from him talking to him during his pitches.

"He says, 'It doesn't bother you talking to me while you're throwing like that?' I said, 'Nah. It's kind of like if you learn your release point then it's just muscle memory. Once you acquire it, I can stand here, look at you, and throw strikes.' He's like, 'You're kidding. Can you really do that?' I say, 'Yeah, I could probably do it blindfolded.' He's standing there, I'm looking him right in the eye and throwing the ball right down the middle of the plate."

Hoyt made an impression, and LaRussa made a somewhat strange pitch to him, asking him to play for him in the Dominican Republic that winter. Hoyt said LaRussa told him he had room for only a Class-A pitcher. It was his way of scouting Hoyt for the AAA White Sox team the next season.

"I knew he was going to be a major league manager one day, too," Hoyt said. "Two days later he calls at six in the morning and tells me I have a flight at the airport waiting on me. So I flew to the Dominican Republic and walk[ed] up to him with my bag about 15 minutes before the game."

LaRussa asked Hoyt if he could start that day, and he said he could as long as there was a uniform for him. He was handed a green uniform that was "the ugliest uniform [he'd] ever seen in [his] life." He just wasn't into the preying mantis look.

It was hot and humid, and Hoyt took only about 10 warm-up pitches before telling LaRussa he was ready to go. LaRussa asked if he was sure and asked if he wanted to know whom he was pitching against. It turned out there were eight major leaguers in the other club's starting lineup.

"I looked over, and I'm thinking we've got these green, crappy-looking uniforms with a big star on them," Hoyt said, "like we're from some kind of sandlot. And this other team looks like the Los Angeles Dodgers. It sort of was. And Tony says, 'This is their Caribbean headquarters. They've got four of their starting players going against you tonight and four other major leaguers.'"

Of course, as was his destiny, Hoyt went to the mound and mowed down all comers. After seven innings, he was pitching a two-hit shutout. LaRussa thought he might be tired from his journey and came out to lift Hoyt. But Hoyt didn't want to leave the mound after flying and starting the ballgame on short notice.

"The least you can do is let me get the last six outs," Hoyt said. "How tough can that be?" LaRussa was not enthusiastic, but Hoyt persisted. "I'll tell you what, if anybody gets on, take me out." LaRussa said, "OK, that's the deal." Hoyt won the game 2–0, and the encounter on the mound was imprinted in his and LaRussa's minds. They were both up with the big club soon after.

"What was funny about it," Hoyt said, "was that it got to be a running joke when we got together on the White Sox. I'd have a game going, and I'd get to the seventh inning against somebody, and Tony would come out of the dugout and he'd say, 'Do you remember that Dominican rule?' I'd say, 'Yeah.' He would say, 'It's in effect.' And I'd go, 'No problem.'"

As soon as Hoyt allowed a base runner after that, he was headed to the showers. If he didn't, he was on his way to a complete game.

Bo Knows Baseball

There was a minute there in the early 1990s when it seemed possible that Bo Jackson would eclipse Shoeless Joe Jackson as the most popular White Sox *Jackson* of all time.

After he emerged as a stud running-back at Auburn University, after he starred in the Los Angeles/Oakland Raiders backfield, and after he poked holes in the walls of the Kansas City Royals' Stadium, Bo Jackson underwent hip surgery. There was no hope of a professional athletic return. Zilch. Not a chance. Not in 1991, 1992, or 1993, but darned if Jackson—just when it seemed hopeless—didn't reinvent himself better than the doctors did and appear as a White Sox pinch hitter and designated hitter.

They said it couldn't be done. After all, senior citizens go under the knife for hip replacement surgery, not in-their-prime athletes. Jackson was a fast healer, ahead of all the game plans for walking, for walking without crutches, for running, and for actually swinging a bat and running on a field. Jackson's comeback was so unlikely that sports-medicine doctor James Andrews advised "ordinary people shouldn't model their activities after Bo Jackson." As if they could before.

Jackson was a phenomenon as he parlayed his great power and speed into dual careers in the National Football League and Major League Baseball (before Deion Sanders considered it). The object of a nationwide marketing campaign, he also led the country in yuks, becoming a running joke for his supposed super-prowess doing anything. Bo knows baseball. Bo knows football. Bo knows cooking barbecue. Bo knows hula hoops.

Jackson made the American League All-Star team in 1989 representing the Royals, and he played parts of two seasons with the White Sox, periodically exciting the masses when he flexed his muscles and drilled a home run into the stratosphere. Before he played again, Jackson was asked how he would know if he was ready. "When I don't have to hold anything back," he replied. "When I'm Bo Jackson again."

The White Sox signed Jackson at the start of the 1991 season with no expectation that he would play a minute for the team before 1992. He fooled everyone by playing 23 games in '91. Anyone who listened to Jackson speak when the Sox inked him, however, should not have been surprised. He was hungry to play ball—any type of ball—again.

"Right now," he said, "I feel like a caged animal. I can't wait for them to open the chutes and let me go and do what I've been doing my whole life, and that's running."

Yet Jackson never really was Bo Jackson again after the surgery. He was never as fast as he had been before the operation nor as consistent, and he went from seemingly indestructible to fragile. He elicited cheers every time he delivered a wondrous clout, but his remarkable comeback didn't last long.

Jackson played in those 23 games for Chicago in 1991 and in 85 games during 1992, slamming 16 home runs. But he migrated to the California Angels in 1993 and retired after that season, a supernova that burned so brightly and burned out so quickly. He was retired by his 32nd birthday.

Ironically, overlapping Bo Jackson's revival with the White Sox was, of all people, Shoeless Joe Jackson, who projected himself into the news from the grave.

An ex-officio body called the Court of Historical Review and Appeals, based in San Francisco, took up Shoeless Joe's case in 1993, and the mock court decided that his permanent banishment from baseball should be overturned and that he should be reinstated. Despite the "ruling," nothing has changed Shoeless Joe's status with professional baseball.

That same year Shoeless Joe, who died in 1951, had a ballpark named for him when it was remodeled in his old hometown of Greenville, South Carolina. Jackson grew up in a house four doors down from the old field.

When Jackson was in his prime, before the Black Sox Scandal of 1919, he averaged .356 and placed great faith in his favorite bat, Black Betsy. Ultimately, about 50 years after Jackson's death, the inherited item was put up for auction.

Making Beautiful Music

Jack McDowell could make both a fastball and an audience hum. He was a Cy Young Award–winning right-handed hitting pitcher and a crowd-pleasing guitarist, and sometimes both at once, it seemed, during his 1990s heyday with the Sox.

McDowell dabbled in rock and roll and made the new Comiskey Park rock when he won 22 games in 1993 and the White Sox captured their division title. McDowell admitted he liked to talk a lot and that it often got him into trouble. He projected cockiness in conversation and on the mound.

Jamming with Pearl Jam, playing late-night sessions in night-clubs, and speaking with frankness and boldness, some felt McDowell might not have been focused enough on his pitching responsibilities. But they were misreading the fires that burned below.

"I've been psychocompetitive for as long as I remember," he said, "so a lot of it has to do with genetics. My entire family is really into sports. When you have that kind of interest, it breeds competitiveness. I'm probably competitive to a fault, but it's been successful for me, so I'd have a hard time convincing myself to change my approach."

Given his interest in music, there were always puns associated with McDowell pitching batters tight. It gave double meaning to "chin music."

McDowell twice won 20 games for the White Sox in a 12-year career that produced a .593 winning percentage. When he left baseball, though, McDowell gravitated to his other love, making music in a band and cutting records. His group was called Stickfigure.

"That's probably one of the funnest parts of being in a band," McDowell said. "Trying to find a name. I liked Stickfigure because it's cool; it's what I think about music and what I'm doing—bare bones."

McDowell said that many people think he must be producing magnitude 9.2-earthquake, punk-rock music "because of how [he] was in baseball." Wrong. "Last time we were on tour [he said in 2004], we got a lot, a lot, a lot of Elvis Costello references. That's good."

At the time McDowell was asked if he would rather have a Cy Young Award or a top-rated hit record.

"I'd rather have a Cy Young because you earn that," McDowell said. "A number one record doesn't mean squat. All that means is you were allowed to get in there, and a bunch of dummies bought your record."

Before that, a bunch of dummies struck out on his fastball.

The Unlikely Big Banger

He was a 6'4", 220-pound mound of muscle, and Ron Kittle brought a slugger's reputation as large as his constitution with him from the minors when he showed up in the White Sox lineup late in the 1982 season.

Competing for the Class-AAA Edmonton Trappers, Kittle swatted 32 homers in his first 72 games. Nice start. He finished with 50 homers and 144 RBIs for the minor league club and was selected as the Minor League Player of the Year. The next season Kittle was not only in the White Sox lineup, he was American League Rookie of the Year.

Kittle's ascent was swift after a slow start. He was cut loose by the Los Angeles Dodgers when he couldn't live up to his billing, but after surgery correcting a pinched nerve, Kittle was tearing it up in the local Indiana leagues. In his early 20s Kittle was playing semi-pro ball in his hometown of Gary in his spare time while making a living as an iron worker for his father, James. Gradually word spread of his hitting prowess, and White Sox pitcher Billy Pierce served as an intermediary for a Kittle tryout. Bill Veeck presided, and Kittle hit the stuffing out of the ball so frequently that the owner immediately signed him.

"I'll bet if he hit 10 balls, seven were in the upper deck and a couple into the lower deck," Pierce said.

Ron Kittle was one of the best and most consistent home-run sluggers ever to play for the White Sox.

Rumor has it that some of the shots still haven't landed.

Kittle could always hit for distance. Growing up, his dad used to reward Kittle for home runs. When he was about 12 he was offered $5 for each home run he belted. That didn't last long, however.

"I hit one, then I hit another," Kittle said. "Then another, and the rate went down to a dollar per home run. Then it went down to a quarter."

Too many home runs too fast.

"The thing is, I was hitting home runs against the good pitchers in the league," Kittle said. "They supplied a little bit more power to hit your bat, and I had better swings. It seemed like every time, even through my big-league career, when I faced a mediocre pitcher, I did horrible against him. It might have just been my attention span. I don't know. Maybe I was a little goofy."

Comiskey Park fans were goofy for Kittle when he became a full-time member of the squad in 1983 and the Sox rushed to a division championship. Kittle clubbed 35 homers with 100 RBIs as a rookie and was selected for the All-Star Game. He was the only White Sox player chosen in the game that marked the 50th anniversary of the first All-Star Game, also played in Chicago. At the end of the season Kittle was voted American League Rookie of the Year, ahead of Julio Franco, who remarkably is still active a quarter of a century later. Franco was playing shortstop for the Indians at the time and is now bidding to extend his major league career into his fifties.

If Kittle had a flaw as a rookie, it was his propensity to strike out. He fanned 150 times that season and joked to a sportswriter that he was "going after the Cy Young, too" because he led the league in strikeouts.

Kittle put together 10 seasons in the majors, retiring in 1991, but he never again topped 35 home runs. He made a better living out of the game than he would have working construction or as an iron worker, but he can't get over how much money players in 2008 make.

"Am I a little jealous that they're making all of this kind of money?" Kittle said. "A little bit, you know, but God bless them. It's changed. I mean some of these guys will never have to work another day in their life."

Although he has been around baseball his whole life in one form or another, Kittle said it is not the love of his life.

"I watch it," he said. "I'm a fan. I never loved the game. I can honestly tell you that. I liked the game. I liked playing it better than I do watching it."

Comiskey I and Comiskey II

When Comiskey Park opened in 1910 it was the greatest sporting palace in the world in the eyes of patron Charles Comiskey, the White Sox founder. It was modeled after the Roman Coliseum, and its designer was nicknamed "the Old Roman," so it fit.

Comiskey Park had staying power. It hosted the first All-Star Game in 1933 and attracted huge crowds in the 1950s when the Sox contended for the pennant and built a fierce rivalry with the New York Yankees. But no building lasts forever with functionality. The Coliseum is still around, but it's a tourist attraction, not an arena for lions devouring hapless prisoners.

When engineers examined Comiskey up close and personal in 1986, it was fraying. "Simply put," an engineer announced, "Comiskey Park is nearing the end of its useful life."

By then White Sox chief owner Jerry Reinsdorf was talking about a new ballpark. The White Sox said if they didn't have a new park for the 1989 season they were prepared to move to a Sunbelt city. Comiskey Park became a political baseball stadium, and amid threats to move the White Sox to Florida if a new stadium was not constructed, plans for a second Comiskey emerged.

As it so happened, a scheme to build anew—across the street from the old park at 35th Street—was revealed by the end of the

1986 calendar year, though the park would not be game-ready until the 1991 season. Already the oldest park in the majors, Comiskey—the building—lived to be 80.

The 1990 season was a nostalgia tour, with old-timers visiting the park one last time before the final game on September 30 and expressing their sadness that it was going away. More than two million fans turned out that season to say goodbye. If attendance had been that good all along, the old park might have stuck around longer. Structural soundness, though, was a growing concern.

"I really hate to see the old lady go," said Luke Appling, the two-decade Sox shortstop.

Tears were shed, the doors were locked, and in the spring of 1991, Comiskey Park reopened. Same name, different structure. The owners were smart enough to bring along an exploding scoreboard to commemorate all of the new Sox home runs and victories in their new house just the way Bill Veeck intended it in 1960.

When the new Comiskey opened (many years before its name was changed to U.S. Cellular Field), fans flocked to the gleaming structure in record numbers. The attendance mark of 2,934,154 was established in 1991, and it lasted until 2006.

With all of the upgrades made over the years since 1991, Comiskey II has surpassed Comiskey I as an impeccable ballpark. If there are tears shed in the stadium now, it is not for memory of the old standard park, but when the White Sox lose a tough game.

chapter 14

Stars of Their Time

Frank "the Big Hurt" Thomas played in 1,959 White Sox games and holds numerous team records to this day.

The Big Hurt

Sometimes when things are too close to you, you don't recognize the significance or importance the way you do with a view from afar. Sometimes living in the moment gets in the way of the big picture.

For that reason some White Sox fans might not realize that the best player who ever suited up in the history of the franchise just left town in 2005, not in 1905. When his contract was up and questions about his health lingered, Frank Thomas packed his bats and moved on to the Oakland Athletics for the 2006 season. And then when that one-year contract ended after a stunningly successful stay, he moved on to the Toronto Blue Jays.

When the day comes that Frank Thomas is tapped for the Baseball Hall of Fame—and that day will almost surely come—he will enter the Hall wearing a White Sox cap.

To read the list of White Sox all-time hitting statistics is to read the history of Thomas's career. The 6'5" slugger (variously listed at 240 to 275 pounds over the years) earned his nickname "the Big Hurt" by putting dents into batted baseballs with the Sox from 1990 to 2005. He played in 1,959 White Sox games, third-most in team history.

Thomas leads the all-time Sox list in the following categories: home runs (448), RBIs (1,465), walks (1,466), doubles (447), extra-base hits (906), and runs (1,327). For a decade and a half, when opponents reviewed the pregame scouting report on the White Sox, pitchers were given carefully thought-out instructions on how to pitch to the Big Hurt in the middle of the batting order.

Few love affairs proceed without some bumps, and the relationship between Thomas, White Sox management, and the fans definitely incurred some heated moments. Thomas sometimes felt he was underpaid and underappreciated. The fans thought he was a crybaby for saying so. Management said it had a team to run and could not merely cater to Thomas's whims.

At the end of the 2005 season, when the White Sox swept to the World Series, Thomas evidenced nothing but joy in being a member of the team even though he could not play beyond late summer because of injury. He had contributed with big blows in the middle of the season when the Sox needed his bat. But when the parade was over, so was Thomas's stay in town. General manager Kenny Williams, unable to count on Thomas's health, cut him loose. So, as so many passionate relationships do, the split between Thomas and the White Sox ended in bitterness.

But there sure was a lot of fun along the way. Thomas was probably the American League's most feared hitter during the middle 1990s, and while it is often recalled that he won two Most Valuable Player awards for the Sox, it is rarely recounted that he won the Home Run Derby at the All-Star Game in 1995. Thomas went head-to-head with Albert Belle, the future White Sox player, in the final round. Thomas's 15 homers during the competition averaged 432.5 feet apiece.

"The MVP is something special," Thomas said. "[But] fans want to see long home runs, so I made sure to hit some very far."

At the time the White Sox were out of the pennant race, and that bugged Thomas, but he put his regular-season emotions aside to get into the spirit of the fan-favorite contest.

"We had some fun, and that's what this is all about," Thomas said.

With the passage of time and the passing of other sluggers into a higher stratosphere in total home runs, some fans have forgotten that it was Thomas who was expected (along with Ken Griffey Jr.) to become one of the top two players of his generation. Crushing the long ball riveted more attention on Barry Bonds, as he passed Hank Aaron to become the all-time home-run king, and on Sammy Sosa and Mark McGwire, who first eclipsed Roger Maris's single-season homer record.

Outspoken on the issue from the start, Thomas shook his head as revelations of steroid and other performance-enhancing drugs took center stage in baseball's world. When he was four or so seasons into his prime, before all the hullabaloo broke out, Thomas was being compared to the game's all-time greats.

White Sox manager Terry Bevington lavished love on his superstar in the manner only a few could explain. In 1995 he said of the still-improving Thomas, "If Babe Ruth was hitting behind Frank, half the teams would pitch to Frank and the other half would walk Frank and pitch to the Babe."

He probably did not mean it quite that way, but at the least that equated Frank Thomas with Lou Gehrig—mighty fancy company.

"I don't know if that's true," added Bevington, who would never have the chance to prove his hypothesis, anyway. "But I believe that."

Also long-forgotten by many is the fact that like Bo Jackson, the supernova superathlete who took the country by storm by playing professional football and baseball simultaneously, Thomas also played baseball and football at Auburn University. He certainly had the build for the gridiron, though if he had thrown himself full blast into football, some coach likely would have remodeled his physique from lean and muscular to big poundage around the middle in order to play offensive or defensive line.

Once, Thomas responded to comparisons between himself and Jackson with a self-effacing nod to the other Tiger.

"You can't compare me with Bo Jackson," Thomas said. "That's just the bottom line. Bo Jackson was probably the best athlete that's ever been. You can't compare me with that guy. I played football and I played baseball at Auburn. He was a superstar in both sports. I was a superstar in baseball but not football. There's no comparison. It's like night and day."

Thomas frequently displayed a smile as wide as the Mississippi River, and he was accommodating to sportswriters who clustered around his Comiskey Park locker. But he was not a player who could disguise his emotions when he felt low or was bothered by things. In 2000—when he went through a difficult divorce, when he first hurt his ankle, when two friends died— Thomas was moody. He occasionally lashed out about working conditions, the Sox, and his contract. He might have ducked into the trainer's room—offering a *no comment* by his absence—but when he was distraught, he was distracted. It may have harmed his play, and it definitely hurt his image.

As a ballplayer ages into his late 30s, things tend to go wrong with his previously well-oiled machine of a body. He is used to functioning on all cylinders, and when a nagging injury pops up— a wrist, a finger, a muscle spasm—he wants to fight through it and ignore it. He can't fathom what's going on. Thomas had to put up with his share of physical woes during his last seasons with the White Sox, including a broken foot twice. No one knew if he would heal sufficiently to become a regular major contributor to the team again.

As it turned out Thomas's body did bounce back. He was able to play at a high level again—but with Oakland and Toronto—after the White Sox turned over their designated hitter job to Jim Thome, another likely future Hall of Famer. Thomas attracted flocks of journalists when he returned to Chicago for the first time with Oakland in 2006 and also with Toronto in 2007. It was clear to those he talked with that he was relaxed, at peace, and if he still harbored resentment towards the White Sox it was confined to Williams, not owner Jerry Reinsdorf.

He expressed pleasure at being back in town, and when he batted with the A's for the first time at U.S. Cellular Field, and the White Sox treated Thomas to a special video-board presentation highlighting his career with the Sox. Fans gave him a standing ovation, and Thomas retaliated with a home run. The fans even clapped for that. It seemed to nicely close a chapter in Thomas's life.

The Blue Jays traveled to Chicago for only one series during the summer of 2007, and the season was well along when Thomas appeared. There was no formal welcome, but fans were gracious, and when he chatted about "life its ownself," as author Dan Jenkins put it, Thomas was at ease and once again said he was glad to be back in Chicago for a visit.

One of Chicago's most distasteful traits is its unrelenting, around-the-clock, unpredictable traffic. Thomas clearly had been away too long because he underestimated the amount of time needed to drive from the northern suburb of Libertyville to the Sox park on the South Side. What logically would take 45 minutes took him more than an hour, and he was late to his locker.

To show that he still appreciated his former superstar employee, Jerry Reinsdorf made a special pilgrimage to the visitors' locker room to visit Thomas.

"It's great that he did that," Thomas said. "Jerry and I buried the hatchet months ago, and it's a good feeling that he did come by. There never was any ill will towards Jerry. Communication was bad with us with the way I left, so it was great to talk with him."

Someone joked that Reinsdorf might have been tipping Thomas off that he was about to trade for him.

"Uh, no, not at all," Thomas said while laughing. "It was just good talking to him. Like I said, we had wonderful years and many meetings and many times talking together, and it's good to talk to him again."

Maybe He Could Have Pitched Forever

It is tantalizing to think just how long Wilbur Wood might have lasted in the majors if he hadn't injured his leg and retired in 1978. Wood is scheduled to turn 67 years old in 2008, and there is still nothing wrong with his arm.

Relying solely on his knuckleball—and with a rule that no one could bunt on him—Wood might be able to pitch a game this year. Certainly, there is no wear and tear on his throwing mechanics. When it comes to discussing great pitching feats of the 20th century, Wood is often overlooked.

Still, as each year passes and as each manager and pitcher shies away from throwing more than 110 pitches per ballgame and barely over 210 innings per season, Wood's accomplishments take on additional luster. His statistics from the mid-1970s are so out of place in modern pitching discussions that they seem to resemble science-fiction baseball. The four-straight 300-plus-inning years with a 376⅔-inning high just make pitching coaches and Xbox-generation throwers laugh out loud.

From his own perspective, Wood, a four-time 20-game-winner, is laughing right back at them while watching his favorite teams, the Red Sox and White Sox, on television in his Massachusetts home.

"This pitch count stuff," Wood said. "They make a federal case out of it. And you didn't have a pitching staff that had 12 or 13 pitchers. It wasn't a five-day rotation like they're doing today, and it wasn't 90 pitches and you're out of the ballgame. Gee whiz....

"There are a lot of guys that can throw more. I don't think pitchers are weaker. They're throwing the ball fast. But if a manager lets his pitcher throw 120 pitches, he stands a good chance of losing his job."

Twice in his 17-year career, Wood finished with earned-run averages below two-per-game. He never got tired and kept trying to tell people that, including his manager, Chuck Tanner.

"I went several times with two days' rest," Wood said. "I did that for, I don't know, maybe 2½ years."

Fleet-Footed Luis

The best baserunner in Chicago White Sox history is immortalized on the left-field wall where the team has imprinted his face and retired jersey number.

Luis Aparicio was the shortstop of the Sox resurgence in the 1950s, succeeding fellow Venezuelan Chico Carrasquel. Yet he did most of his talking with his feet. When it comes to consistency, baseball rewards performances that register at a high level year after year. Well, the 10-time All-Star recorded an achievement that few have accomplished in any of the sport's statistical categories. Aparicio led the American League in steals nine straight years, beginning in 1956.

Nine years in a row Aparicio went unchallenged. It was a time period when the long ball was in ascendancy and not many teams focused on taking the extra base by playing small ball. Fans *oohed* and *ahhed* when Mickey Mantle or Willie Mays hit a home run, but

Luis Aparicio, the best base runner in White Sox history, is immortalized on the left-field wall of U.S. Cellular Field.

fewer gave credit to the speedster who disrupted a pitcher's motion. The big bang has been in fashion ever since, though many practitioners of the art of stealing have made their mark.

At 5'9" and 160 pounds (and some may dispute the listing in *The Baseball Encyclopedia*), Aparicio would have been an unlikely power hitter. He used the skills that best suited his body to advance around the bases 90 feet at a time rather than in one 360-foot circle with a single stroke of the bat.

Since so few teams focused on stealing bases, Aparicio led the American League with only 21 in his rookie year. However, four times he stole more than 50 bases in a season, with a high of 57 and a career total of 506. He was a singular weapon for the aptly named Go-Go White Sox, with skipper Al Lopez relying more on pitching, fielding, and manufacturing runs than he might have with the power-hitting New York Yankees.

During his 18-year career, Aparicio connected for 2,677 hits, one of the greatest totals ever by a shortstop, so he did much of the heavy lifting to put himself on base in position to steal. While he accurately predicted that he would be able to play for a long time, Aparicio just as accurately predicted he would not be able to reach the milestone of 3,000 hits when he passed 2,000 at age 35.

"That would take another seven years," Aparicio said. "But I do believe I can play as a regular for at least four more years."

Aparicio made that comment in 1969 and retired in 1973. When Aparicio came to the United States he was not fluent in English. His knowledge of the language improved, but he was often shy around interviewers. When he retired as a major league player, Aparicio did not stay around the game in the United States. He still spends most of his time in Venezuela and makes only periodic appearances in the U.S. to sign autographs at baseball-card shows and for White Sox events.

In 1984 Aparicio was elected to the Hall of Fame in Cooperstown, New York, and in the summer of 2006 a statue of Aparicio and the late Nellie Fox completing a double play was unveiled at U.S. Cellular Field. Except for those instances he has rarely spoken to spectators on his quick visits north.

Aparicio also made a special cameo appearance for the White Sox when the team passed out its 2005 World Series rings near the start of the 2006 season. As it so happened, the date virtually coincided with the 50th anniversary of Aparicio's first appearance in the White Sox lineup.

Southpaw Billy Pierce pitched the game, and another famous newcomer played for the Sox for the first time on April 17, 1956. Larry Doby, the first African American to play in the American League, had come over from the Cleveland Indians.

White Sox catcher Sherm Lollar and second baseman Fox took the young Aparicio under their tutelage, offering pointers in the field, but also educating the soon-to-be-22-year-old on what it took to be a major leaguer.

"Especially Sherman," Aparicio said years later of the wisdom the late Lollar imparted. "He really helped me in showing me the attitude I should have for the game. When I broke in I got a lot of help from him and Fox. I don't think I would have made it if it wasn't for them. I had just gone from two years in the minor leagues, and now I come to the big leagues. But their attitude to me was great."

From afar, baseball fans of the 1950s and 1960s acknowledged Aparicio as the king of the base path. But those who studied the game the closest—his teammates—were just as awed by his acrobatics with a glove. Center fielder Jim Landis said he was sometimes paralyzed watching the great stops Aparicio made when he should have been running to back him up.

In 1955 it was believed that the designated successor to Carrasquel might be a young man named Sammy Esposito. Esposito said he was released from the Army and reported directly to minor league Memphis. Esposito saw Aparicio stop every grounder and make every throw and realized if he wanted his career to advance he had better make a quick change.

"I see this little guy bouncing around, making throws and everything," Esposito said in 2006. "It was Aparicio. And I said to myself, 'Uh, oh. I'm at the wrong place here.'" When Esposito was introduced to the players and was asked what his position was, he immediately said, "Third base."

Although top-notch Venezuelan players have worn a path to the majors with regularity since, Aparicio was still a rarity when he broke in. But he came from good genes, and the adult males in his family had long before made an impact on the game in the baseball-mad country.

Aparicio always praised his father's and uncle's influence on his career and on getting him interested in playing baseball at a young age. "They took me to the ballpark often, and each helped me a lot," he said.

When he was growing up, Aparicio idolized Carrasquel and then-future White Sox shortstop and manager Ozzie Guillen idolized Aparicio.

When he does talk about the highlights of his major league career, Aparicio always returns to 1959. It was the pivotal season for a generation of ballplayers and fans, the time the White Sox went to the World Series and had a chance to bring home their first crown in 40 years.

"1959 was an unbelievable year," Aparicio said. "To win a pennant you've got to have at least 10 or 15 guys have good years. And that's what happened with us."

It is a memory shared with all longtime White Sox fans who also look back on 1959 as a very good year.

chapter 15

The 21st-Century Sox Unlimited

Usually good-humored Sox manager Ozzie Guillen, shown here joking around with his players in the dugout at U.S. Cellular Field on September 15, 2007, has come to symbolize the 21st-century Sox.

The Bronzed Catcher

If Carlton Fisk had his way he would have been installed permanently behind the plate at Comiskey Park rather than being immortalized in bronze in center field.

Fisk was the embodiment of the catcher position. He was tough, played hard, was a leader on the field and in the clubhouse, and never wanted to peel off the chest protector and shin guards. The Hall of Fame catcher played in the majors from 1969 to 1993, 24 seasons split between two colors of Sox. He came up with the Red Sox and played with Boston through 1980, and he played the second half of his career in Chicago. He was tremendously admired and beloved in both towns.

Fisk never was much for displaying sentimentality, but when the White Sox approached him to let him know that they wished to raise a statue commemorating his achievements in Chicago, he was dumbfounded. Upon the statue's unveiling in August 2005, he was even a little bit emotional.

"It doesn't matter how long you've played," he said, "the statue is forever, and that's what's mind-boggling."

An 11-time All-Star, Fisk slugged 376 home runs and appeared in 2,499 games. He wanted to catch forever and thought he had earned that right, so his parting from the White Sox in 1993 when he was released even as a 45-year-old, was bitter. Worse, it came in the middle of the season, so when the Sox released him, Fisk quietly disappeared on a road trip from his hotel. He hadn't been playing much, and the Sox wanted to break in younger catchers.

Fans were none too happy at the sight of Fisk on the bench, nevermind after he was cut. Signs were displayed at the ballpark reading, "Pudge Deserves Better."

Eventually, though Fisk kept to himself, was somewhat estranged from the team, and was removed from the limelight, he got better. In 2000 he was chosen for membership in the National Baseball Hall of Fame. The recognition touched his soul.

"I think getting this is probably more of a complete and deep satisfaction than I could ever express in words," Fisk said. "To have my adult children and their families be a part of me and what's happening today, maybe allowed me to act like a kid in front of my kids."

He was both giddy and thoughtful as he toured the Hall prior to his induction.

"I never sought recognition or justification," Fisk said. "I won't say that I marched to the beat of a different drummer, but I did have my own path, and I usually blazed my own trail."

In 2003 Fisk participated in a catcher's forum discussion with CNBC newsman Tim Russert. He, Yogi Berra, Johnny Bench, and Gary Carter, all Hall of Fame receivers, talked about the position. Once again Fisk went public for a rare moment, offering intriguing insights into his relationship with pitchers.

"I always felt as though—as being a catcher—I was in control of the game," Fisk said. "I was in control of the pace of the game. I wanted to control my pitching staff. Sometimes we didn't have the best pitching staff, so I had to control his emotions and try to get him to give me his best. So, it was all in an effort to win the game."

By the time the White Sox commissioned a statue of Fisk, his memorable No. 72 jersey had also been retired. At the time, the White Sox had erected statues of team founder Charles Comiskey and outfielder Minnie Minoso. Fisk appreciated the gesture.

"I'm not sure if I can express it," he said of his emotions. "This is the second-best feeling I've had in baseball. One was putting on the Hall of Fame ring on the day I was inducted, and the other is today."

White Sox owner Jerry Reinsdorf, who was the pivotal figure in acquiring Fisk through free agency after he purchased the team, called the player "one of the cornerstones of a White Sox history that has existed for more than a century. He has always had an enormous following among White Sox fans, and it is appropriate to recognize him for all of the amazing memories and lasting impressions he left with the fans of Chicago."

Ozzie Stops Talking

Always possessing a fan-friendly image, especially given the influence of onetime owner Bill Veeck, the White Sox conducted a fan giveaway of manager Ozzie Guillen bobblehead dolls in the middle of the 2007 season.

The voluble Guillen got a sneak peak at the figure—which was a good likeness—and had one on a shelf behind his desk in his U.S. Cellular Field office the day before the official handout to fans. Guillen was asked if he was going to gather up a large number of them to stage his own giveaway to friends and family members. He said he wasn't sure yet because they might be too expensive.

"It all depends if they pay me," Guillen laughed. "There's a lot of people I know in Venezuela."

Yet he knew some Guillen family members would definitely be asking for one, and Guillen knew he better come up with them for some people.

"Yeah, my mom," he said.

It was raining outside, and it looked none too promising for the White Sox to get their game in that night (although after considerable delay the event was played). Guillen pontificated on weather and its effect on players, pitchers in particular. Something not unlike Abbott and Costello in *Who's on First?*

"Sometimes it's cold, and you want to blame the cold for the game," he said. "You feel better another day, and they call the game off. A rain delay is no help to anybody. The weather is a big factor in this game. You are gonna see good weather only maybe 30 games out of the whole 162. That's all you know that's going to be nice. Some days it's gonna be too hot or too humid or too cold. It's gonna rain; it's too windy. Perfect days, there are only going to be maybe 30 of them. When the perfect day comes, you've got to take advantage of it. Football's different because I don't know if they stop a game for anything. It's just a different game."

Neither Guillen nor the White Sox could imagine what would happen the next day when the bobbleheads were dispersed. The

White Sox had a bad game, and Guillen was in an exasperated mood when he met the media. He showed up in the interview room holding an Ozzie bobblehead—with its mouth taped shut.

It was a more eloquent statement about the manager's feelings on the game than anything he could have said.

You Can Go Home Again

Outfielder–first baseman Rob Mackowiak was born in Oak Lawn, Illinois, just outside of Chicago, and when he was obtained in a trade with the Pittsburgh Pirates in December 2005, he was thrilled to go to the hometown team. So was his family. So were his friends. They gobbled up tickets to watch Rob play.

"At first a lot of them came," Mackowiak said. "It was a lot of fun, actually, because you got to see a lot of family and a lot of friends who hadn't had the chance to see you play."

Mackowiak's previous appearances as a major leaguer in Chicago were in games at Wrigley Field against the Cubs. Wrigley often sells out, making it more difficult to find enough seats to accommodate the whole gang.

"You only get so many tickets," Mackowiak said. "Wrigley is a difficult place to leave all of your family tickets, so it was definitely cool to be able to do it with the White Sox. I was definitely a little bit nervous at first. Most of them had never seen me play besides in college or high school. You're running down the sidelines [toward right field] before the game, and there are all these people you know waving. It was kind of, 'Oh, God, they're all here to watch me.' So definitely there was a little bit of nervousness."

Mackowiak had fun playing in his hometown, though he said not all ballplayers are quite so loose about it.

"I've heard bad stories, too," he said. "There are a lot of people who have been playing at home that make it sound like a doomsday thing. I enjoyed it. It's what you make of it, I guess. You've got to separate the on-field and off-field stuff. Your family wants to be around you. In 2006, just after the World Series, it was tough.

Everybody is trying to pull you their way, your buddies from college [South Suburban Illinois Junior College] and high school. This year [2007] it's been a lot calmer."

Separating his professional and personal lives was the key for Mackowiak.

"That's the ticket to life," he said. "I changed my phone number last year, and that was half the battle right there, getting rid of the number."

The family, be assured, still has his current number. Mackowiak didn't shut them out of his games.

The Big One That Got Away

It is said that White Sox catcher A.J. Pierzynski is a magnet for controversy on the field. Whether it be hard-nosed plays at the plate, making his opinions known in discussions, or running into other guys while trying to take an extra base, Pierzynski is a fiery player.

One thing he does to relax on the rare off-days during the season is go deep-sea fishing. It has become an annual ritual for A.J., friends, and sometimes teammates or White Sox personnel if the Sox have time on a West Coast swing, to chase the biggest fish in the sea. Pierzynski, who loves salt-water fishing, also fishes for tarpon and snook in Florida waters and has caught marlin and dolphin.

During the summer of the 2007 season, such a chance arose when the Sox were moored in the Los Angeles area. Pierzynski and pals embarked on a shark-fishing adventure.

"You just want to get away from baseball for a day or two, basically," Pierzynski said. "It gives you a chance to think about something else instead of thinking about baseball, how you're going to get a hit, and stuff like that."

Four fishermen headed out on the Pacific Ocean, and three sharks were caught right away.

"One right after the other," Pierzynski said. "One of them was big, probably 150 or 200 pounds, and seven feet long or so. It

White Sox superstar A.J. Pierzynski, seen here celebrating the Sox's 2005 World Series victory, was not so victorious on a shark-fishing trip in 2007.

was a good one. That looks very big, especially when it's a shark."

Then came Pierzynski's turn. Using Spanish mackerel as bait and dropping it about 25 feet beneath the surface, the catcher felt a fish tugging on his line. He reeled, and the line took off. Pierzynski reeled some more, and the fish fought. The captain let him know that he had something pretty big on the line.

This fish did not want to go gently into the good night. Time passed with man and shark battling, pulling with all their might. The captain figured the fish weighed between 300 and 400 pounds. Pierzynski is 6'3" and weighs 240 pounds, so he was battling on closer to even terms than many other humans would be. Most top-notch athletes do some weightlifting to tone their muscles, and Pierzynski was quizzed on how pulling back on the rod with that type of dead weight compared to hitting the gym and lifting.

"It was a little bit different because in weightlifting you take a break," Pierzynski said.

No breaks in fishing when a big one is on the line. Any slackening of resistance, and the catch is sure to pull back and regain line it has lost in the struggle.

"You're pretty much locked in," Pierzynski said. "You have a belt on [to help keep the angler's back straight], and the captain was saying most people go for about 20 minutes and then give up. But there was no way I was giving up the rod."

Pierzynski said he felt the captain was serious about him surrendering the fight after 20 minutes. Pierzynski wanted to prove himself of sterner stuff than the majority, and besides, he was surrounded by friends he was sure would tease him about the missed opportunity for the rest of his life if he gave up so easily.

"My friends were there, and I wasn't about to let go," Pierzynski said. "They would talk about it. They would talk about it all the time."

An hour passed, and neither the caught fish nor the catcher would give ground. Another hour passed, and, although he was tiring, Pierzynski held on. The entire epic adventure was starting to approach "The Old Man and the Sea" proportions.

The Hundred Years War culminated at the three-hour mark. Suddenly, the line twitched, the shark squirmed, and the big monster escaped into the deep, leaving a disappointed A.J. with no fish for his troubles. For some reason the fish got off the hook.

"There's nothing you can do," Pierzynski said. "That's why it's called fishing, because you don't catch every one. We don't know why, really, it got off. Even the captain couldn't believe it. He said, 'You did everything right. You've fished before.' So he really didn't have any idea. It's all about timing, being in the right place at the right time."

And even if you never let go, the fish might beat you anyway.

He's Seen the White Sox from Both Sides Now

Greg Walker played all but 14 games of his major league career with the White Sox, ending in 1990. In 2007 he completed his fourth season as the team's hitting coach. So he has been both management and player with the franchise that he loves, but when he reviews all of those years wearing white and black, he first thinks of the friendships made.

"The things that stand out to me really in my career are the people that I've met," Walker said. "I was very fortunate when I broke into the big leagues [in 1982] to be with one of the greatest coaching staffs ever put together. Tony LaRussa was the manager. Jim Leyland was the third-base coach. Eddie Brinkman was my infield instructor. Charley Lau was the hitting coach. Art Kusnyer was the bullpen coach, and he's still here. Dave Duncan was the pitching coach.

"There's the great players, Carlton Fisk, Tom Seaver, and other guys who might not be household names. I could go on and on about the people. You just get to be such close friends with these guys. They're your family. We were together for a long time. The training staff, too. Head trainer Herm Schneider is one of my favorite friends in the world. The relationships were what I missed most when I retired and stayed out of baseball for 10 years."

Hitting coach Greg Walker (right) makes Scott Podsednik laugh during 2006 spring training. Walker played for the Sox for many years and then became their hitting coach in 2004. Photo courtesy of AP/Wide World Photos.

The manager is the point man for the team in Major League Baseball, and sometimes coaches are overlooked. Some are on their way up, on their way to taking over their own club, but some are content to spend years tutoring players without seeking their own managerial slot. From his vantage point as a coach now, Walker has fresh eyes on the men who helped him 25 years ago. But as a young man did he realize their strengths and wisdom then?

"These guys were so good it was pretty obvious at the time," Walker said. "I mean, if you had Charley Lau as your hitting coach you knew you had the best. Tony LaRussa and Jim Leyland, with these guys you're talking about two of the great managers of all time. And Dave Duncan is one of the great pitching coaches of all time. Art Kusnyer should be in the Hall of Fame for coaches. So it was obvious early on that that was a special group of people, though I don't think anybody knew they would go on to the success they had."

Possessing such reverence for the famed coaches he played under, Walker admits their influence remains strong in him today, and he thinks of many of their comments when he works with current Sox hitters.

"Every day," he said. "And not just the coaches, but the players I played with. The reason this game is sustained is because it is passing it down the line. One reason I wanted to get back in the game was that some really good people helped me to think about the way to go about your business, and I think that's very important.

"The game is passed down the line from generation to generation of players. Hopefully, these guys [the current White Sox] will do the same thing. And I think that's what makes baseball what it is."

The White Sox are one team that has worked hard to bring back loyal players in roles with the team after they have retired. Manager Ozzie Guillen was once the club's star shortstop. Coach Harold Baines's jersey number is retired. Coach Joey Cora played for the Sox. Walker said he feels he is fighting to succeed with old comrades who have been through the wars with him before.

This kind of talk resonates with longtime baseball fans that grew up with the sport and followed their hometown teams for years. When the team claimed the 2005 championship, it had been 88 years since the White Sox won a World Series title. Walker thinks fans definitely are part of the same continuum, as a team progresses from decade to decade.

"You hear about that kind of support from people, and it really became evident when we won the World Series in '05 and they went downtown to the parade," he said. "All the fans and all the people who came up to you afterwards talked about the first game they went to with their grandfather. They said they were going to go out to the graveyard with their programs and read it to them. You realize what makes baseball special."

chapter 16

World Series Champs...at Last

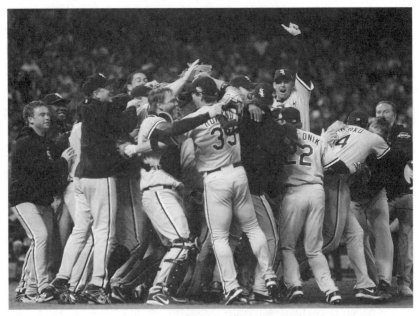

The Chicago White Sox celebrate after winning Game 4 of the 2005 World Series against the Houston Astros at Minute Maid Park in Houston, Texas, on October 26, 2005.

The Impossible Dream Becomes Reality

As the 2005 season wore on, the improbable became possible. The Chicago White Sox had appeared in only one World Series since the infamous 1919 Black Sox Scandal. The White Sox had not won a World Series championship since 1917. It had been 88 years, and generations of White Sox fans had gone to see their maker without witnessing their favorite ballclub win it all.

Except for a late-season blip when it seemed the Cleveland Indians might overcome their deficit in the American League Central Division standings, the White Sox owned their division, were in possession of their own destiny. Ozzie Guillen, the fast-talking, blunt, humorous manager, once a popular shortstop for the team, seemed to inject just the right amount of energy and spark whenever it was needed.

His lineup performed superbly, with sluggers such as Paul Konerko and Jermaine Dye providing pop, Joe Crede devouring grounders at third base like the second coming of Brooks Robinson, and newcomers Tadahito Iguchi and Scott Podsednik adding bunting prowess and speed on the base paths. On the mound, starters Jon Garland and Mark Buehrle were difference makers, and late-arriving summer call-up Bobby Jenks anchored the bullpen.

Sometimes teams seem snakebitten by injuries, dissension, and contract distractions. Sometimes every button the manager pushes is the right one. The summer of 2005 was such a season for Guillen and the White Sox.

The Sox finished the season with a 99–63 record and six games ahead of Cleveland.

Although the Indians made the Pale Hose nervous in the last month of the campaign, the Sox led the division by 15 games on August 1. They were not giving away the title.

"You know, it took so long for Chicago to get back in there, it just felt like there was so much—I don't know if I want to say *pressure*, but there was so much *emphasis* on, 'This is our chance,'" first baseman Konerko said. "It was, 'If we don't win this, it might take another 100 years to even get back here.' It was definitely do or die, and I think that wound up giving us the edge."

By winning the Central Division crown the White Sox moved on to the American League Division Series against the Boston Red Sox. The Red Sox were the defending world champs, having exorcized their own Babe Ruth–inspired demons in 2004. By winning the World Series for the first time since 1918, the Red Sox had wiped out the Curse of the Bambino, the alleged voodoo spell that hovered over the team for more than 80 years following the sale of Babe Ruth to the New York Yankees. The White Sox were trying to shove aside the curse of the Black Sox Scandal.

The White Sox swept the Red Sox—not nearly as well-rounded a club as they had been a year earlier—in three games to advance to the American League Championship Series. Then came the remarkable dazzling of the California Angels when the Sox captured four of five games. In the series opener at U.S. Cellular Field, Billy Pierce, the southpaw star of the 1950s, threw out the ceremonial first pitch.

It was one day the Sox might have considered signing him to a short-term contract since the Angels won, 3–2.

But after losing the opener, the Sox's Buehrle, Garland, Freddy Garcia, and Jose Contreras hurled consecutive complete-game victories.

And then to wrap it all up the Sox faced down and dominated the Houston Astros, sweeping the first Texas team to ever play in a World Series, 4–0.

"No matter who we played in that World Series," Konerko said, "with the exception of playing the Cubs, there was nobody who could have matched the urgency that we had. Everybody was just so focused and intent. There wasn't like any off time or down time between games. Every waking moment we just focused on getting it done. We knew how great it would be. We also knew that if it didn't happen, it would be such a letdown for people. I mean for about 20-some days it was literally I don't remember sleeping. I also don't remember being tired. It was just such an unbelievable time. If I had to go back and do it all over again to get back there, it wouldn't be the same."

October baseball was a rarity for the White Sox, and after playing so well for the months leading up to autumn, it indeed would have been a bummer for Sox fans if the team had not come home carrying the winner's trophy.

Chicago is a living, breathing baseball rivalry, 365 days a year. There are Cubs fans and White Sox fans, and people who grew up in the city picked an allegiance early in life, often because of the view adopted by their family. It is like coming from a Democratic or Republican family.

However, in the fall of 2005, there was more than crispness in the air. The undecideds—general baseball fans without ties to the Cubs and who might have grown up elsewhere—were definitely tilted toward the Sox. Lukewarm White Sox fans showed their colors by waltzing down Michigan Avenue with caps and T-shirts. It was one of the most glorious times in baseball history to be a White Sox fan.

Although the playoffs seemed lopsided, the entire outcome could have changed on a little thing. The play was magnified by the circumstances, and it is not forgotten, though it was swept away by a tidal wave of subsequent events. The Sox dropped the League Championship Series opener to the Angels, and Buehrle survived Game 2, 2–1. How the Sox scored the winning run will live forever in Sox lore.

The White Sox were staring at extra innings when catcher A.J. Pierzynski came to the plate in the ninth inning. The hard-hitting catcher had a strong season and endeared himself to Sox fans with his scrappy play. On this at-bat, it appeared Pierzynski struck out swinging. Angels catcher Josh Paul rolled the ball back to the mound as if A.J.'s K was strike three. Only, Pierzynski ran to first in the manner of a batter who feels the third strike was dropped. Umpire Doug Eddings never signaled strikeout and ruled that A.J., not Paul, was right.

Pinch-runner Pablo Ozuna stole second and scored the winning run on a double by Joe Crede. Suddenly, Pierzynski was viewed as smarter than Albert Einstein.

It was a stunning turnaround and momentum-breaker for the Angels. Instead of the Angels being ahead 2–0 in the series, it was deadlocked 1–1. The Sox swept the next three games and celebrated like it was 1917.

"You always think you can win one," said Konerko, who stroked 40 home runs with 100 RBIs that season. "You're always trying. Every year you start off, you hope you're going to get to the play-offs, and in the back of your mind you almost have a feeling it might never happen, so winning it all, it was kind of one of those things where I can die in peace no matter what happens if you get another hit, another home run, or if you never do anything ever again."

Konerko, nicknamed Paulie by the Chicago fans who chant his name that way when he is introduced at the plate, said only a small percentage of baseball players will be remembered in the game because of their greatness and will then proceed to the Hall of Fame. The others who cannot aspire to enshrinement and immortality that way can claim a piece of it by playing with a winner, by playing for a World Series champ that is always remembered for its team achievement.

"Everybody was just proud," Konerko said. "Superstar players, regardless of whether they win or not, Hall of Fame guys, they're going to be remembered. But I think for most of us who are in the middle, guys who are making a living playing the game for a number of years who might not be remembered otherwise, we're going to be remembered by winning. And that's the way it should be. You should be remembered for winning."

Professional athletes in all sports speak often of "winning the ring." The championship ring cements the good feeling of the result; it is the prominent souvenir token to have and hold, to save and show off, for the remainder of a player's life. It is the most precious of remembrances.

The White Sox championship-ring ceremony was conducted at U.S. Cellular Field early in the 2006 season. Some players already traded away returned for the occasion. The White Sox not only gave away replicas of the gaudy baubles to fans, they choreographed a ceremony with the rings being carried to the pitching mound by an army of tuxedo-clad bearers.

Every player, every season, begins spring training with the hope and dream that he will earn the right to watch such a ceremony and wear such a ring. Owning a World Series ring is a stamp of approval. But wearing one takes judgment and tact. Not every player wears a World Series ring everywhere he goes. And active players like to think they are going to earn a matched set with another title.

Konerko said he does not wear his World Series ring around the house, to the beach, to casual events in Bermuda shorts, but likes to wear it when he dresses more formally with a sport coat.

"I wear it occasionally when we travel on the road," Konerko said. "We have to dress up, and also we're in a team atmosphere. I don't like wearing it in situations where no one would know who I was. That brings attention to it, and it's kind of like bragging a little bit. I think maybe it's one of those things where I'll wear it more when I'm done playing.

"I'm going after another one, so I'll just try to win the next one. If it doesn't happen, I'll wear the first one a lot when I'm retired."

Given how many years the White Sox paid penance from the 1919 scandal to the 2005 World Series, a little bragging wouldn't hurt much. And believe it, White Sox fans did their share of bragging—and rubbing it in—after the victory, to Cubs acquaintances.

Four of a Kind

The Houston Astros were regarded as a team that could never win the big one in the playoffs. When the Astros met the Sox, it was a milestone for the Houston franchise, born in 1962 as the Colt .45s and the team that gave the world the Astrodome, the first domed stadium for a major league American club. But not even Nolan Ryan could have saved the Astros against the Sox.

The White Sox not only displayed superior pitching and clutch hitting, they also got timely hits from unlikely suspects. When leadoff hitter Scott Podsednik blasted a game-ending, ninth-inning home run to capture Game 2, 7–6, it was apparent that the Sox were a team of destiny. The speedy left fielder had hit zero home runs during the regular season.

Then late-season pickup Geoff Blum, another toothpick-wielding hitter, whacked the decisive homer in a 7–5, 14-inning triumph in Game 3. There is little doubt each swat will be the most important in each man's career.

Blum, a journeyman acquired at the July 31 trading deadline from San Diego for a minor league player, was known for his versatility in the field, not for the power in his bat. He hit only one regular-season homer for Chicago in limited playing time. If the game had not lasted so long, it's doubtful Blum would have had his chance, and he was as pleased and surprised as anyone that he contributed a big-situation homer.

"I didn't know if I got it high enough," Blum said. "Somebody was watching out for me."

Podsednik made his mark with the Sox as a base-stealer, though he will be long-remembered for his walk-off homer in Game 2. The count was 2–1, and Podsednik was expecting a fastball from Houston pitcher Brad Lidge, an All-Star closer. Podsednik felt Lidge had to come in to the plate and was waiting.

"I said, 'Hey, let's put a good swing on this fastball,'" Podsednik said later. "It was a good pitch to hit, and I was able to drive it out."

The big hits were symbols of the way the season went for the Sox. The right player in the right situation at the right time delivered. Really, who knew that Bobby Jenks would be the savior of the season? In fact, in spring training and through the first half of the season, who knew about Bobby Jenks at all?

Righty Dustin Hermanson owned the Sox's closer role, and there was no clamor for change. Hermanson posted 34 saves with a 2.04 earned-run average, but back problems sidelined him and could have spelled ruination for the Sox's season if it had not been for the surprising arrival of Jenks.

The 6'3", 270-pound Jenks was a monster on the mound with a fastball that occasionally touched 100 mph. He was reminiscent of the great Boston Red Sox closer of the 1960s, Dick Radatz.

Sometimes manager Ozzie Guillen signaled the bullpen for Jenks's use not by tapping his right arm to give him the right-hander, but by making a large circle with both hands, signifying Jenks' roundish supersize. Not only did Jenks pick off six saves with a 2.75 ERA in the regular season while stepping in for Hermanson, but he was the last man standing for the last out in the World Series when the Sox ended their 88-year drought. Captured in photographs, it was his leap into the air, with arms held high that epitomized the joy of the Sox.

Jenks was unwanted by the Angels, who felt he had limited potential, not to mention off-field problems. He has since blossomed into a full-fledged All-Star.

Guillen, who was named American League Manager of the Year, mixed and matched his lineup with genius all year, and it all worked. The first Venezuelan major league manager, wildly popular at home already, became the toast of his home country.

"If I ran for president, I'd have a shot," Guillen said shortly after hoisting the World Series trophy, "because I'm in the news every day. I'm popular. They don't want to bring me in because I know my politics, but because I'm popular.

"No, I wouldn't want to be a California governor. Not California or Florida. There's a lot of stuff that happens there every day—earthquakes, fires, immigration. That's a lot of work. I don't want to be governor. They have too many problems to deal with."

Problems besides the other team's hit-and-run or southpaw coming out of the bullpen.

Stepping Up Big Time

Right fielder Jermaine Dye had been a successful, solid hitter and all-around player with the Kansas City Royals and the Oakland Athletics, and 2005 was his first year with the Sox. The addition of his bat firmed up the lineup. Dye hit 31 home runs and drove in 86 runs.

But his most impressive contributions came during the World Series against the Astros. Dye hit .438 and was selected as the Most Valuable Player. For a year after that, a life-sized photograph of Dye was on display at the National Baseball Hall of Fame and Museum in Cooperstown, New York. Alas, Dye never got the chance to go see himself in the place of honor.

"I was there for the Hall of Fame game when I played with Kansas City," Dye said, "but I haven't been back there since." Dye laughed at the notion that he should telephone the Hall and see if they will give him his long, tall portrait.

"I haven't collected much in the way of souvenirs in my career," Dye said. "I do have my first home-run ball and stuff like that. I gave my stuff—a bat, a ball, a jersey and shoes that I wore—to the Hall of Fame. What you have is a lot of memories. You have memories of going to the World Series and winning the World Series. That's your dream. That's why you play this game, to win the World Series. There are a lot of memories that go with it."

The most vivid and important memory of the Series for Dye is his eighth-inning single in Game 4 that sent Willie Harris home with the winning run in a 1–0 game that clinched the title.

Dye played a strong Series, but several White Sox players contributed mightily to the cause, so it was not a foregone conclusion that he would win MVP honors. When his name was announced as the recipient of the trophy, Dye was caught off guard a bit.

"I was excited," he said. "We had a bunch of guys who could have won it. I was just hot at that point of time for a couple of times, and you know there's nothing more exciting than winning the World Series, but to be selected as MVP was a great accomplishment, too."

Ozzie Guillen fostered a close-knit team that relied on excellent starting pitching, complemented by the big bats of a handful of players. Others added speed and top-notch fielding. The White Sox were an unspoiled team of guys who wanted to do something special.

"This is a totally different type of team than any other team I've been on," Dye said. "This is the way you're supposed to play the game. What we have here is pretty good: speed at the top of the lineup, a balanced mix of power and good defense. We'll hit and run. We'll do the little things. That's the way you play the game.

"We don't have any egos on this team. I think that was what was really special about this club."

Dye, who used to be an avid bass fisherman, but has transferred his outdoors focus to hunting, certainly does not wear his World Series ring when he goes out in the woods. Much like Konerko, he said he wears it with dressy clothes.

"When you first get it you wear it a bit, then it kind of gets stored and is sitting around," Dye said. "I think once I'm done playing, that's probably when the memories will really set in. You'll look back on some things and talk with a bunch of guys and tell lies and stuff like that."

In the case of Dye and the White Sox, however, the story of 2005 is a pretty good truth.

A Second-Life Championship

When the 1917 White Sox won the World Series, they were acclaimed as the greatest team of all time. When the 1919 White Sox threw the World Series, they were decried as the worst team of all time. The lifetime suspension of eight White Sox players by commissioner Kenesaw Mountain Landis decimated the team for years.

Yet no one would have imagined that it would take 40 years, until 1959, for the White Sox to again play in a World Series. And none alive in 1917 would have predicted it would take 88 years for the Sox to win the World Series again.

The 2005 champions were the champions for generations of White Sox fans, but also for White Sox players. Luke Appling never played in a World Series. Nellie Fox, Luis Aparicio, Billy Pierce, Jim Landis, and famed manager Al Lopez represented the Sox in 1959, but they couldn't outplay the Los Angeles Dodgers.

Lopez was still alive when the White Sox made their magical run in 2005 and was gleeful when they swept the Astros. Only days after the White Sox won the crown, Lopez died at age 97.

White Sox management was generous with former players, inviting them to see the two Series games in Chicago, involving them in activities and giving former players like Pierce and Minnie Minoso their own World Series rings. It was a big-hearted gesture by owner Jerry Reinsdorf. The gifts were a symbol that those former players were also a part of the Sox's triumph.

For Guillen and coaches like Harold Baines and Greg Walker, winning the Series title had even more meaning. They had played on successful White Sox teams that had not advanced to the Series. This was a second chance for them.

Sox hitting coach Greg Walker was a first baseman for the team in the 1980s and played on the 1983 team that won the division title but lost in the playoffs. To earn a ring in his 40s that he couldn't in his 20s was humbling.

Not until after the Game 4 victory over Houston, not until after the clubhouse whooping died down, not until the city of Chicago threw a parade, did Walker realize how much the 2005 team's championship meant to so many people who never spent a minute in the club's uniform.

"I knew it was important," Walker said. "But when it really hit you how important it was in this town was during the parade.

"We knew as a team we had accomplished something, and all that is great, but when we came into town and saw the people at the parade and how they came up to you and told you how much it meant to them and their fathers and grandfathers, that was something. It didn't happen once. It happened a thousand times if it happened one time.

"And you know, whatever happens from now on, you know you played a small part of it as a coach. I helped in a little way to give this city a World Series championship. And I'm very thankful for it. I'm thankful for our players for going out and fighting for it. I'm thankful for our ownership and our management for giving me a chance. They're the best."

Everyone Loves a Parade

Chicago is a city that loves its professional franchises, from the Bears to the Bulls, from the Blackhawks to the Cubs and White Sox. Fans with long memories and long allegiances live in the city and its surroundings. Yet championships are not so common (except for the six won by the Michael Jordan–era Bulls) that they are spoiled.

In fact, given the last time the Chicago Cubs won a World Series was 1908, the last time the Blackhawks won the Stanley Cup was 1961, and the last time the Bears won a Super Bowl was at the end of the 1985 season, Chicago sports fans are pretty much championship-deprived and championship-starved.

So when the city declared, "Let's throw a parade!" after the White Sox won it all in 2005, the fan base was hardly jaded. The White Sox attendance was around 2.3 million, and the parade attendance was around 2 million, according to the office of Mayor Richard M. Daley.

A ton of confetti was thrown. A mob of fans sometimes stood 20-deep to watch the heroes of the moment pass by in a motorcade of five trolleys and six double-decker buses. The journey of celebration began appropriately at U.S. Cellular Field and passed through Bronzeville, Chinatown, Pilsen, and on to downtown.

Pitching star Mark Buehrle said the crowds gave him a continuous thrill.

"This is the greatest feeling of my life right here," he said. "From the moment I left U.S. Cellular Field to here I had goose bumps the whole way."

During the ceremony Paul Konerko made his owner, Jerry Reinsdorf, cry by giving him the ball from the final out in the fourth game in Houston. It was a feel-good day for everyone except Cubs fans hunkered down in bunkers out of sight.

Near the end of the 2006 season, Reinsdorf revealed that for months he received thank-you letters from longtime White Sox fans who sometimes said they were also writing in behalf of

Approximately two million people turned out for the White Sox's victory parade through downtown Chicago on October 28, 2005.

long-dead relatives. The World Series championship meant that much to them.

"After we won," Reinsdorf said, "it turned out to be something far different than I thought." By winter, he said, "what I came to realize is the honor I had in playing a role that made literally millions of people happy. If I die today, at least I played that role."

Guillen seemed to sense that even before anyone wrote a word.

"Thank you guys for waiting so long," Guillen trumpeted to the fans at the parade gathering. "Thank God we did it for you guys."

Maybe because his Bulls were supposed to win with superstar Jordan and because so few gave his White Sox a chance to win, Reinsdorf seemed more affected by winning a World Series than he was by winning NBA titles. On this occasion before the masses, he said, "This is absolutely the most fantastic day of my entire life."

Fans skipped out on work, and parents let kids skip out on school to be part of it all. Nobody could afford to risk the chance that they were missing out on a once-in-an-every-88-years party.

epilogue
Immortalized in Bronze

This statue of legendary White Sox pitcher Billy Pierce was unveiled at U.S. Cellular Field on July 23, 2007.
Photo courtesy of Ron Vesely/Chicago White Sox.

The sun was bright and strong as it bore down on the center-field concourse at U.S. Cellular Field in midsummer. Billy Pierce wore a red rose in the lapel of his light-brown sport coat and used a handkerchief to dab at sweat forming on his forehead.

Decked out in a complementary-print golden tie, the old south-paw was dressed for a special occasion. One of the most popular players in the history of the Chicago White Sox franchise was being accorded a special tribute on July 23, 2007. The team was unveiling a statue of the 1950s star, bestowing a rare and special honor.

Folding chairs were arrayed in a blocked-off area for the pregame ceremony in the hour before the White Sox took on the Detroit Tigers, Pierce's first major league team. A cloth—a black and gray White Sox blanket—covered the Billy Pierce statue that was joining the pantheon of replicas of other key figures in White Sox history. The special collection of statues symbolizes important individuals in team annals. Team founder Charles Comiskey was so honored. So was Hall of Fame catcher Carlton Fisk, longtime star Minnie Minoso, and the double-play combination of the late second baseman Nellie Fox and shortstop Luis Aparicio. Pierce was in good company.

Among the White Sox luminaries in attendance were owner Jerry Reinsdorf, former general manager Roland Hemond, Minoso himself, and ex-players like Bill Melton, Ron Kittle, Jim Landis, and Jim Rivera. The two Jims, Pierce's old teammates, remain Pierce's best friends from the old days when the Sox fought their way to the 1959 World Series. Kidding around, Kittle raised two fingers in a *V* formation to create rabbit ears behind Melton's head.

They were all joined by numerous members of the Pierce clan—Pierce's wife, Gloria, who had a corsage pinned to the jacket of her blue pants-suit; children Bill, Patti, Bobby, and Bob; and grandchildren Erin, Jaci, Zack, Billy, and Sean. All were hemmed in by White Sox fans straining to see the activities and record them on cameras while enduring the blazing sun. A bouquet of roses was presented to Gloria, and the compliments flowed as one man after another spoke from the heart about the seven-time All-Star's stay with the White Sox between 1949 and 1961.

As an inspirational choice, when it came time for music to be played, the Sox piped in "Go-Go White Sox." The song alone provokes pleasant memories of the Billy Pierce era. For a moment, former players lined up with arms on each other's shoulders and high-kicked like the Rockettes.

Pierce was called, "one of the greatest to ever wear a White Sox uniform" and "one of the best pitchers of his era and one of the most consistent pitchers of any era."

Pierce was also lauded for his efforts to raise $12 million in charitable contributions since 1970 as chairman of the Chicago Baseball Cancer Charity.

A countdown, 5-4-3-2-1, was spoken, and then the cloth was whipped off the statue. There was vintage Billy Pierce in full windup. The sun was in the real-life Pierce's eyes at the time, however, and he shielded them with his right hand in order to see himself. Then the player took over the microphone and thanked everyone from Reinsdorf and the Pierce family to the batboys and the fans of the 1950s.

"To me," Pierce said, "the best year I had was 1949."

Not only did he become a member of the White Sox, but Pierce got married that year, too. He offered a nod to the fielding prowess of Jim Landis, Jim Rivera, and Minnie Minoso, all ex-teammates, thanking them for all the help they gave him.

"They chased down all my mistakes," Pierce said.

Pierce was moved by the installation of the statue—just as he had been when his number was retired.

"This is such a tremendous honor for me," he said while smiling broadly. "A person could not ask for anything more, and to have my family here makes it even more special. I can sneak up here once in a while and come see it."

Pierce watches the White Sox on television all the time and does so with a critical eye, predicting plays and manager's calls. Sometimes he will tell his wife that a bunt is called-for, and if he gets it right, she says, "Well, you should know that. You were in it long enough." Sometimes Pierce is wrong about the upcoming action. "If I'm wrong, she won't say anything."

Pierce attends a half dozen or more White Sox games a season just as a fan. When he comes to games incognito, Pierce indulges in ballpark food, typically ordering two hot dogs with onions to satisfy an appetite that belies his trim waist. This from a man who has a concession stand named after him at U.S. Cellular Field.

The convivial affair broke up in the outfield after about 20 minutes, and former players, fans, and Pierce family members exchanged greetings.

"He deserves 20 statues," said Ron Kittle, the White Sox slugger of the 1980s and early 1990s. "He's such a nice man."

Pierce was whisked away from the friendly mob temporarily so he could throw out a ceremonial first pitch. Pierce, who had turned 80 around opening day, no longer burns in 90 mph fastballs. His concession to age when invited to throw out first pitches nowadays is standing in front of the mound instead of on the rubber, and he said he warned the White Sox he would do it that way. Pride is wounded if a former player bounces his throw, and the embarrassment is doubled if the former player is a pitcher. Figuring that he never practices anymore and that his motion could result in a bounced toss to the plate, Pierce has adapted.

"I've got new rules," said Pierce, who threw to White Sox left-handed pitcher John Danks. "Now I stand real close. I started doing that about two years ago."

That is the type of old-age admission that former teammates normally would pounce upon and tease a buddy about mercilessly. Yet Landis, 73, and Rivera, 85, let him off the hook.

"I accused him of dogging it," Landis said, "but now no one would care."

After completing all of his official duties, Pierce, his family, and friends retreated to a White Sox skybox for a party.

"To me, this is very special," said Landis, who flew to Chicago from California to be present for the statue's debut. "He was a great pitcher."

Rivera, who lives in Indiana, within a couple of hours driving distance from the ballpark, said he wouldn't miss the occasion.

"He deserves it," Rivera said. "It was always a great pleasure to play behind him."

As he reflected on the day's happenings with a wide smile, Pierce removed his tie.

"Oh, it was hot out there," he said.

Pierce saw the statue at various stages of its sculpting, but had not seen the finished version before the public did, not until the moment the White Sox cloth was removed.

"The last time I saw it, it was headless," Pierce said. It had improved in the interim. "I was excited. It looked very nice. I was kind of flustered and excited, but I did get a good look at it. It was very thrilling. To have my family there and friends—these are my friends, and it's nice to be with them."

Earlier in the same season, Pierce threw out a first pitch for a nearby minor league team, and the club honored him by giving fans a bobblehead doll of him in uniform. Pierce got one, too, and placed it on the mantle in his living room. However, Gloria said it didn't look like him. The model for the young Billy Pierce of the statue, though, was a photograph that Pierce has in his basement. The statue, in his mind, does him justice.

"Oh yes, it looks like me," he said.

One of Pierce's grandsons was playing on a summer baseball team, and his teammates obtained tickets to the game. Stationed in the outfield stands as play unfolded, they rose, stripped off their shirts, and revealed the name *Billy Pierce* painted on their bare chests. Pierce laughed about it when he saw the display.

In the bottom of the fifth inning, an in-house camera panning the stadium located Pierce sitting in the front row of his skybox-for-the-day, intently watching play. When he realized he was on camera, Pierce waved to the crowd. He was beaming. There seemed no doubt that on another day, the fans who saluted Pierce might well find him strolling through the statues in center field, gazing upon his own likeness and recalling glory days of White Sox play gone by.

notes

Chapter 1

Beginnings

"Gee, I can...": Axelson, G.W., *Commy: The Life Story of Charles A. Comiskey* (Jefferson, NC: McFarland & Co., Inc., 2003), p. 5.

"Then take the damn thing...": Brown, Warren, *The Chicago White Sox* (Kent, OH, Kent State University Press, 2007), p. 69.

Hitless Wonders

"He has palm-leaf ears...": Kessler, Gene, "Nick Altrock, the Ed Wynn of Game, Just Wiggles Ears and Goes Ahead Drawing Big Pay for His Clowning," Unidentified newspaper, The National Baseball Hall of Fame Library Archives, Oct. 5, 1933.

"If I had a mouth full of...": Kessler, Gene, "Nick Altrock, the Ed Wynn of Game, Just Wiggles Ears and Goes Ahead Drawing Big Pay for His Clowning," Unidentified newspaper, The National Baseball Hall of Fame Library Archives, Oct. 5, 1933.

"Is that your schnozzle?": Kessler, Gene, "Nick Altrock, the Ed Wynn of Game, Just Wiggles Ears and Goes Ahead Drawing Big Pay for His Clowning," Unidentified newspaper, The National Baseball Hall of Fame Library Archives, Oct. 5, 1933.

"Don't you gentlemen...?": Kessler, Gene, "Nick Altrock, the Ed Wynn of Game, Just Wiggles Ears and Goes Ahead Drawing Big Pay for His Clowning," Unidentified newspaper, The National Baseball Hall of Fame Library Archives, Oct. 5, 1933.

Spitball man

"I never had any trouble with Ty...": Monardo, Frank, "Pitching Only 30 Pct. Now–Walsh," *The Sporting News,* January 9, 1957.

"The ball is too lively...": Broeg, Bob, "A St. Pat's Salute to Ed Walsh," *The Sporting News,* March 24, 1979.

"Livelier balls, smaller ballparks...": Schabo, Joe, "Ed Walsh Sees Life Like Game," *Fort Lauderdale News,* May 26, 1959.

"I'll remember as long as I live...": Holtzman, Jerome, "Big Ed Walsh, 77, Former White Sox Star, Gets Day to Remember at Comiskey Park," *The Sporting News,* July 2, 1958.

Chapter 2

Around the World

"Why not...": Brown, Warren, *The Chicago White Sox* (Kent, OH, Kent State University Press, 2007), p. 39.

"He didn't even notice...": Brown, Warren, *The Chicago White Sox* (Kent, OH, Kent State University Press, 2007), p. 42.

"A most useful...": Brown, Warren, *The Chicago White Sox* (Kent, OH, Kent State University Press, 2007), p. 46.

"glorified rounders...": Brown, Warren, *The Chicago White Sox* (Kent, OH, Kent State University Press, 2007), p. 52.

Red Faber, Spitball Man II

"Maybe it seemed that way...": Cooper, Brian E., *Red Faber: A Biography of the Hall of Fame Spitball Pitcher* (Jefferson, NC: McFarland & Co., Inc., 2007), p. 7.

"Where the hell are you going?": Cooper, Brian E., *Red Faber: A Biography of the Hall of Fame Spitball Pitcher* (Jefferson, NC: McFarland & Co., Inc., 2007), p. 79.

"Urban Faber is my....": Cooper, Brian E., *Red Faber: A Biography of the Hall of Fame Spitball Pitcher* (Jefferson, NC: McFarland & Co., Inc., 2007), p. 185.

"I've never seen a team...": Carmichael, John P., "Rowland Calls '17 ChiSox Best Club of All Time," *The Sporting News,* August 26, 1959.

"Nobody could have cracked...": Carmichael, John P., "Rowland Calls '17 ChiSox Best Club of All Time," *The Sporting News,* August 26, 1959.

The Black Sox Scandal
"Cicotte Bares...": Unbylined, unidentified newspaper clipping, The National Baseball Hall of Fame Library Archives, October 30, 1919.
"Everybody knows...": Unbylined, unidentified newspaper clipping, The National Baseball Hall of Fame Library Archives, October 30, 1919.
"I'm particularly sorry...": Williams, Joe, "An Echo of 1919 Sell Out; One of the Fixers Speaks: A Hit Batter the Tip Off," *New York World-Telegram,* unidentified date, The National Baseball Hall of Fame Library Archives.

Chapter 3

Shoeless Joe Never Forgets
"I was playing in Anderson...": Unbylined, unidentified, undated, clipping from The National Baseball Hall of Fame Library Archives, about 1916.

A Lion on the Mound
"If I were managing...": Fay, William, "A Straight Lyons," *The Chicago Sunday Tribune,* about 1947, undated, The National Baseball Hall of Fame Library Archives.
"Old Ted's been paroled...": Fay, William, "A Straight Lyons," *The Chicago Sunday Tribune,* about 1947, undated, The National Baseball Hall of Fame Library Archives.
"I never heard Ted...": Holtzman, Jerome, "Lyons Friends Recall His Special Greatness," *Chicago Tribune,* July 27, 1986.
"Except on the day...": Holtzman, Jerome, "Lyons Friends Recall His Special Greatness," *Chicago Tribune,* July 27, 1986.

More Stars than the Night Sky

"There will be no more tickets...": Ward, Arch, "All Bleacher Seats Are Sold in 45 Minutes," *Chicago Tribune,* July 4, 1933.

"We wanted to see the Babe...": De Luca, Chris, "The Game of the Century," *Chicago Sun-Times,* July 15, 2003.

Bucketfoot Al

"Leave the young man alone...": Associated Press, "Al Simmons, 54, Dies Suddenly," May 26, 1956.

"Of course, I've heard...": Graham, Frank, "Simmons' Spirit Fires Sox," *The New York Sun,* May 27, 1933.

"More young men should be playing baseball...": Graham, Frank, "Simmons' Spirit Fires Sox," *The New York Sun,* May 27, 1933.

Junior Tried To Be Like Dad

"Baseball owes you...": Shannon, Paul H., "Big Ed Walsh Climbs Back Into The American League Again—As Umpire," *Boston Sunday Post,* January 1, 1922.

"I have strength...": Shannon, Paul H., "Big Ed Walsh Climbs Back Into The American League Again—As Umpire," *Boston Sunday Post,* January 1, 1922.

"I want him to have...": Adams, Franklyn J., "Young Ed Walsh and What He Means to Old Ed Walsh," unidentified newspaper, The National Baseball Hall of Fame Library Archives, December 13, 1928.

Chapter 4

Shortstops Need Not Apply

"He was pretty raw...": Graham, Frank, "Indestructible Shortstop," *Collier's,* July 9, 1949.

"When I saw a pitch...": Povich, Shirley, "Appling: They Came No Better," January 5, 1991.

"Gomez was pitching...": Lapides, George, "Two Decades Later, Luke Appling Is Still a Crowd Pleaser," *Memphis Press-Scimitar,* April 25, 1979.

"Never made an error…": Edwards, Henry P., American League
  Service Bureau press release, December 10, 1933.
"Not a chance…": Edwards, Henry P., American League Service
  Bureau press release, December 10, 1933.
"It's nice to be…": Holtzman, Jerome, "Appling Coming Back
  Home–ChiSox Fans Delighted," *The Sporting News,*
  October 25, 1969.

Street Smarts, Not book Learning

"I submit…": Smith, Red, "Shoeless Joe's Letter Reader," *The
  New York Tribune,* February, 1947, unidentified specific date,
  The National Baseball Hall of Fame Library Archives.

Bargain Pickup

"It was the best break…": Whitney, Eugene, "Bust With Tribe,
  Lee Travels on 20-Victory Road," August 10, 1941, unidenti-
  fied newspaper, The National Baseball Hall of Fame Library
  Archives.
"I couldn't keep…": Whitney, Eugene, "Bust With Tribe, Lee
  Travels on 20-Victory Road," August 10, 1941, unidentified
  newspaper, The National Baseball Hall of Fame Library
  Archives.

Fingers in the Dykes

"Be yourself…": Edwards, Henry P., American League Service
  Bureau press release, January 31, 1937.
"We slept on…": Dykes, Jimmie, and Charles O. Dexter, *You
  Can't Steal First Base* (New York, J.B. Lippincott Co., 1967),
  P. 21.
"We slept late…": Dykes, Jimmie, and Charles O. Dexter, *You
  Can't Steal First Base* (New York, J.B. Lippincott Co., 1967),
  p. 21.
"Dear Madam…": Dykes, Jimmie, and Charles O. Dexter, *You
  Can't Steal First Base* (New York, J.B. Lippincott Co., 1967),
  p. 71.

"Where would you...": Dykes, Jimmie, and Charles O. Dexter, *You Can't Steal First Base* (New York, J.B. Lippincott Co., 1967), p. 77.

"Who the heck...": Dykes, Jimmie, and Charles O. Dexter, *You Can't Steal First Base* (New York, J.B. Lippincott Co., 1967), p. 87.

"A manager should...": Edwards, Henry P., American League Service Bureau press release, January 31, 1937.

"I hate to tell you...": Unbylined, unidentified short, The National Baseball Hall of Fame Library Archives, May 19, 1938.

Chapter 5

The Go-Go White Sox

"I took Looie...": Tybor, Joseph, "Sweetness at Short: Chico Carrasquel," *Chicago Tribune,* July 8, 1990.

"I came from a baseball-playing...": Forman, Ross, "Little Looie," *Sports Collector's Digest,* June 28, 1991.

"Chico was my idol...": Forman, Ross, "Little Looie," *Sports Collector's Digest,* June 28, 1991.

"I've never seen him play...": Van Dyck, Dave, "Guillen Shrugs Off Aparicio Label," *The Sporting News,* April 29, 1985.

You have to say...": Kahn, Roger, "Little Nellie's A Man Now," *Sport,* April 1958.

"Nothing doing...": Kahn, Roger, "Little Nellie's A Man Now," *Sport,* April 1958.

"What?": Kahn, Roger, "Little Nellie's A Man Now," *Sport,* April 1958.

"Yeah...": Kahn, Roger, "Little Nellie's A Man Now," *Sport,* April 1958.

"It's nothing...": Kahn, Roger, "Little Nellie's A Man Now," *Sport,* April 1958.

"Of all the stars...": Munzel, Edgar, "They Call Fox Biggest Little Guy in Game," *The Sporting News,* September 4, 1957.

"He was so eager...": Munzel, Edgar, "They Call Fox Biggest Little Guy in Game," *The Sporting News,* September 4, 1957.

"I didn't like baseball…": Callen, Bill, "Fox Tracks Lead to Hall," *The Times-Union,* unidentified date in 1997, The National Baseball Hall of Fame Library Archives.

"Where is St. Thomas?": Kahn, Roger, "Little Nellie's A Man Now," *Sport,* April 1958.

Forever Is a Long Time

"I fight because I …": Bring Buck Back Organization press release, 2003.

"For heaven's sake…": Bring Buck Back Organization press release, 2003.

"Buck Weaver was…": Bring Buck Back Organization press release, 2003.

"I played baseball…": "Buck Weaver Dead at 64; Denied 'Black Sox' Charge," January 31, 1956, Unbylined, unidentified clipping, The National Baseball Hall of Fame Library Archives.

El Señor

"Just one game…": Lindberg, Richard C., *The White Sox Encyclopedia* (Philadelphia, Temple University Press, 1997), p. 67.

"If we had a stopper…": Munzel, Edgar, "'White Sox Were Stopped Only by Lack of a Stopper'—Senor," *Chicago Tribune,* October 25, 1957.

"Al could best…": Prell, Edward, "Al The Man Equal of Al the Manager," *Chicago Tribune,* September 23, 1959.

"His name…": Johnston, Joey, "Lopez 'Was Tampa Baseball,'" *The Tampa Tribune,* October 31, 2005.

"At Chicago…": Associated Press, "Senor Al Realizes a Dream" (in *St. Petersburg Independent*), February 1, 1977.

"He is certainly making…": Unbylined, "Limit Contract To One Year," *The Chicago Daily News,* September 29, 1959.

"I'm *anti*…": Goldstein, Richard, "Al Lopez, a Hall of Fame Manager, Is Dead at 97," *The New York Times,* October 31, 2005.

The Third Fielder Up the Middle

"What could I...": Johnston, Joey, "Lopez 'Was Tampa Baseball,'" *The Tampa Tribune,* October 31, 2005.

"It may sound...": Microsoft Corporation, Undated interview with Jim Landis, The National Baseball Hall of Fame Library Archives.

Chapter 7

Veeck—as in Laughs

"One of my...": Frank, Stanley and Edgar Munzel, "A Visit With Bill Veeck," *The Saturday Evening Post,* June 6, 1959.

"This may be heresy...": Frank, Stanley and Edgar Munzel, "A Visit With Bill Veeck," *The Saturday Evening Post,* June 6, 1959.

"Baseball serves...": Frank, Stanley and Edgar Munzel, "A Visit With Bill Veeck," *The Saturday Evening Post,* June 6, 1959.

"No bigger than...": Frank, Stanley and Edgar Munzel, "A Visit With Bill Veeck," *The Saturday Evening Post,* June 6, 1959.

"When you can't laugh...": Furlong, William Barry, "Master of the Joyful Illusion," *Sports Illustrated,* July 4, 1960.

The American Way

"We are hoping...": Munzel, Edgar, "Veeck Exercises His Option in Deal to Control ChiSox," *The Sporting News,* February 25, 1959.

"He can't be...": Carmichael, John P., "Calm Sportshirt Lets Ship Drift, Asks Chuck Aboard," *The Sporting News,* April 1, 1959.

"I am...": Munzel, Edgar, "'I'm Running Club,' Comiskey Tells Veeck—Bill Turns Cheek," *The Sporting News,* April 1, 1959.

"I'm just here...": Munzel, Edgar, "'I'm Running Club,' Comiskey Tells Veeck—Bill Turns Cheek," *The Sporting News,* April 1, 1959.

"If we want fans...": Munzel, Edgar, "'I'm Running Club,' Comiskey Tells Veeck—Bill Turns Cheek," *The Sporting News,* April 1, 1959.

"Chicago is my…": Furlong, William Barry, "Master of the Joyful Illusion," *Sports Illustrated,* July 4, 1960.

"A one-time…": Veeck, Bill and Murray Robinson, "I Know Who's Killing Baseball—Every Man for Himself With Club Owners," *The Cincinnati Post,* August 13, 1958.

"Who needs…": Veeck, Bill and Murray Robinson, "I Know Who's Killing Baseball—Every Man for Himself With Club Owners," *The Cincinnati Post,* August 14, 1958.

"Some of…": Frank, Stanley and Edgar Munzel, "A Visit With Bill Veeck," *The Saturday Evening Post,* June 6, 1959.

"It makes good…": Unbylined, unidentified clipping, The National Baseball Hall of Fame Library Archives, August 5, 1958.

Practice What You Preach

"I want you to…": Furlong, Bill, "Dad's Work Rubbed Off on Veeck," *The Chicago Daily News,* February 19, 1959.

"It's not the size…": Unbylined, "Whatta Day! Moms at Sox Game Agree," *The Chicago Daily News,* May 11, 1959.

"The White Sox…": Duck, Harvey, "Veeck Dreams Up New Gimmicks to Lure Fans," *The Pittsburgh Press,* June 28, 1959.

"I love him…": Unbylined, "Whatta Day! Moms at Sox Game Agree," *The Chicago Daily News,* May 11, 1959.

Chapter 8

The Little Left-Hander

"When Billy Pierce…": Burns, Ed, "Pierce Paces Hose Pitchers on Control," *The Sporting News,* June 6, 1951.

"Paul nursed me along…": Burns, Ed, "Pierce Paces Hose Pitchers on Control," *The Sporting News,* June 6, 1951.

"I soon got the idea…": Daley, Arthur, "The Hardluck Kid," *The New York Times,* March 15, 1956.

"They always…": Greene, Jamal, "Billy Pierce, Lefthanded Ace," *Sports Illustrated,* March 19, 2001.

Chapter 9

The Man of the Hour

"He's got...": Holtzman, Jerome, "Rubber-Wing Wynn Restores
  Snap When Sox Start to Sag," *The Sporting News*,
  September 23, 1959.

"I had to prove it...": Holtzman, Jerome, "Rubber-Wing Wynn
  Restores Snap When Sox Start to Sag," *The Sporting News*,
  September 23, 1959.

"I'll keep going as long...": Holtzman, Jerome, "Rubber-Wing
  Wynn Restores Snap When Sox Start to Sag," *The Sporting
  News*, September 23, 1959.

"Maybe I can pitch...": Holtzman, Jerome, "Rubber-Wing Wynn
  Restores Snap When Sox Start to Sag," *The Sporting News*,
  September 23, 1959.

"I'll bet...": Holtzman, Jerome, "Rubber-Wing Wynn Restores
  Snap When Sox Start to Sag," *The Sporting News*,
  September 23, 1959.

Better with Age

"Now you tell me...": Holtzman, Jerome, "Like Vintage Wine,
  Wynn Improves as Years Roll By," *The Sporting News*,
  August 5, 1959.

"After all...": Holtzman, Jerome, "Like Vintage Wine, Wynn
  Improves as Years Roll By," *The Sporting News*, August 5,
  1959.

"His breaking stuff...": Munzel, Edgar, "Victory No. 250 for
  Wynn Whets Desire for More," *The Sporting News*, April
  22, 1959.

Winning When Others around You Are Losing

"The fellows all hustle...": Rumill, Ed, Undated, unidentified
  article, The National Baseball Hall of Fame Library Archives.

"Hey, Gus...": Kahn, Roger, "Early Wynn's Struggle," *Sport*, July
  1962.

Going After 300

"I figure…": Richman, Arthur, "Frisky and Forty, Wynn Sets 300 Goal," Unidentified publication from spring training 1960, The National Baseball Hall of Fame Library Archives.

Chapter 10

World Serious

"This World Series…": Prell, Ed and Edgar Munzel, "Gun With 40 Years of Rust Explodes in Dodgers' Faces," *The Sporting News,* October 14, 1959.

"We're a better…": Munzel, Edgar, "Go-Go White Sox Slowed to Crawl in Dodger Park," *The Sporting News,* October 14, 1959.

Trader Bill

"Any pitcher…": Heiling, Joe, "Every Pitcher Wants to Win 20— But Tommy John Will Settle for 15," *The Sporting News,* March 5, 1966.

"If you were…": Heiling, Joe, "Every Pitcher Wants to Win 20— But Tommy John Will Settle for 15," *The Sporting News,* March 5, 1966.

A 1960s Instant Replay

"I didn't want…": Munzel, Edgar, "Senor Puts Squeeze on Servers to Raise Their Victory Sights," *The Sporting News,* March 2, 1963.

"Maybe if I had…": Holtzman, Jerome, "Silent Man Landis Sounds Off—Sees White Sox on Rise," *Chicago Sun-Times,* March 14, 1964.

"I quit…": Holtzman, Jerome, "Silent Man Landis Sounds Off— Sees White Sox on Rise," *Chicago Sun-Times,* March 14, 1964.

New Slugger on the Block

"I've never hit...": Munzel, Edgar, "...a 4-HR Salvo" (headline cut off in The National Baseball Hall of Fame Library Archives), *Chicago Tribune,* July 12, 1969.

"I just didn't...": Munzel, Edgar, "...a 4-HR Salvo" (headline cut off in The National Baseball Hall of Fame Library Archives), *Chicago Tribune,* July 12, 1969.

Auld Lang Syne

"I leave without regret...": Stevens, Bob, "Pierce Gave Much to Baseball," *San Francisco Chronicle,"* October 5, 1964.

"We took separate...": Associated Press, January 21, 1965, appeared in *The New York Times* of the same date.

"For goodness sake...": Associated Press, February 3, 1965, unidentified clipping, The National Baseball Hall of Fame Library Archives.

"I admit I did wrong...": Falls, Joe, "Eddie Cicotte–at 81, He's Proud of Life He's Led; Family Is, Too," *The Sporting News,* December 4, 1965.

"I've tried...": Falls, Joe, "Eddie Cicotte–at 81, He's Proud of Life He's Led; Family Is, Too," *The Sporting News,* December 4, 1965.

"I tell...": Falls, Joe, "Eddie Cicotte–at 81, He's Proud of Life He's Led; Family Is, Too," *The Sporting News,* December 4, 1965.

"We're going...": Munzel, Edgar, "Little Looie Sees ChiSox Grabbing Division Crown," *The Sporting News,* April 19, 1969.

"Really, I believe...": Munzel, Edgar, "2,000 Hits for Looey, Still a ChiSox Pillar," *The Sporting News,* May 31, 1969.

"You know what?": Munzel, Edgar, "2,000 Hits for Looey, Still a ChiSox Pillar," *The Sporting News,* May 31, 1969.

Chapter 11

Veeck—as in Back

"Love me…": Mullen, James C., "Veeck Elegance: Sox Hot Pants!" *Chicago Sun-Times,* March 10, 1976.

"I would use…": Mullen, James C., "Veeck Elegance: Sox Hot Pants!" *Chicago Sun-Times,* March 10, 1976.

"I'm not worried…": Mullen, James C., "Veeck Elegance: Sox Hot Pants!" *Chicago Sun-Times,* March 10, 1976.

"Hell, no…": Mullen, James C., "Veeck Elegance: Sox Hot Pants!" *Chicago Sun-Times,* March 10, 1976.

"One girl…": Mullen, James C., "Veeck Elegance: Sox Hot Pants!" *Chicago Sun-Times,* March 10, 1976.

"Hopefully, not on…": Mullen, James C., "Veeck Elegance: Sox Hot Pants!" *Chicago Sun-Times,* March 10, 1976.

"Sometime, somewhere…": Veeck, Bill and Ed Linn, *Veeck—As in Wreck* (Chicago: University of Chicago Press, 2001), p. 380.

"I'm very flattered…": Holtzman, Jerome, "Executive of Year—White Sox Savior Veeck," *The Sporting News,* November 12, 1977.

The South-Side Hitmen

"I can't wait…": Dozer, Richard, "ChiSox Sowed Zisk Trade Seeds in September," *The Sporting News,* undated, The National Baseball Hall of Fame Library Archives.

"It's been a fantastic year…": Holtzman, Jerome, "'Fantastic Year' in Comebacks by Soderholm, Veeck," *The Sporting News,* October 22, 1977.

"Having guys like…": Madden, Bill, "The Finley Deal That Turned into A 'Lemon,'" *Baseball Quarterly,* date indistinguishable, The National Baseball Hall of Fame Library Archives.

A Slugger Emerges

"It smells funny…": Holtzman, Jerome, "ChiSox Quaff Champagne—Toast Homer Champ Melton," *The Sporting News,* October 16, 1971.

Fluttering to Success

"Everybody thinks...": Holtzman, Jerome, "Workhorse Wood–
King of White Sox Hurlers," *The Sporting News,* October 2,
1971.

"Everybody keeps asking...": Holtzman, Jerome, "Workhorse
Wood–King of White Sox Hurlers," *The Sporting News,*
October 2, 1971.

"I've thrown a knuckleball...": Munzel, Edgar, "Wilbur Apt Pupil of
Old Prof Wilhelm," *The Sporting News,* May 6, 1967.

"I need all that weight...": Munzel, Edgar, "Wood's Knuckler a
Mystery to A.L. Batters," *The Sporting News,* June 2, 1973.

"It's not Jim Kaat...": Dozer, Richard, "Kaat's Quick Release
Handcuffs Sox Rivals," *The Sporting News,* May 31, 1975.

"Shucks...": Dozer, Richard, "Kaat's Quick Release Handcuffs
Sox Rivals," *The Sporting News,* May 31, 1975.

Disco Demolition Fame and Flames

"It was just such....": Mitchell, Fred, "Kessinger recalls
'Unbelievable' Disco Night," *Chicago Tribune,* July 13, 2006.

"This was almost...": Sullivan, Paul, "A Memory That Will Never
Be Demolished," *Chicago Tribune,* July 9, 2004.

"For years...": Veeck, Mike and Pete Williams, *Fun Is Good*
(Rodale Books, Emmaus, PA: 2005), p. 85.

Chapter 12

Richie Allen or Dick Allen?

"I hope I'm worthy...": Durso, Joseph, "Dick Allen, in a Landslide,
Is Voted American League's Most Valuable," *The New York
Times,* November 16, 1972.

"I like to hit...": Associated Press, "Holy Cow Homer in Holey
Underwear," August 24, 1972, The National Baseball Hall of
Fame Library Archives.

"No, never in my life...": Associated Press, "Mom's Grin Tells It
All: Dick in Chi Having a Ball," appeared in *Binghamton
Sunday Press,* April 22, 1973.

"This is hard for me…": Dozer, Richard, "Allen Bids Adieu to ChiSox Fame, Fortune," *The Sporting News,* September 28, 1974.

A Corker

"They didn't have to wine…": Weinberg, Rick, "Content: Happy to be Out of Cleveland, Albert Belle Looks to Erase His Former Misfit Image," *Sport,* May 1997.

"My standard line…": Weinberg, Rick, "Content: Happy to be Out of Cleveland, Albert Belle Looks to Erase His Former Misfit Image," *Sport,* May 1997.

"Chicago is a great place…": Weinberg, Rick, "Content: Happy to be Out of Cleveland, Albert Belle Looks to Erase His Former Misfit Image," *Sport,* May 1997.

Orta Just What Was Ordered

"I'm not a good…": Hillyer, John, "Orta His Own Severest Critic as .315 Hitter," *The Sporting News,* August 31, 1974.

"Mannerisms at the plate…": Hillyer, John, "Orta His Own Severest Critic as .315 Hitter," *The Sporting News,* August 31, 1974.

"He always tries…": Hillyer, John, "Orta His Own Severest Critic as .315 Hitter," *The Sporting News,* August 31, 1974.

Double-Duty DeBusschere

"Breakfast and dinner…": Waldmeir, Pete "DeBusschere Juggles Hoop, Diamond Careers," *The Sporting News,* March 2, 1963.

"He tells…": Waldmeir, Pete "DeBusschere Juggles Hoop, Diamond Careers," *The Sporting News,* March 2, 1963.

Everything Ventured, Everything Gained

"A neighbor said…": Battista, Judy, "If Bases Are Filled With Mets, Ventura Becomes Tougher," *The New York Times,* May 22, 1999.

"The times you try...": Battista, Judy, "If Bases Are Filled With Mets, Ventura Becomes Tougher," *The New York Times,* May 22, 1999.

"When it happened...": Stark, Jayson, "Ventura's Horrible Fall Will Haunt White Sox," *The Philadelphia Inquirer,* March 25, 1997.

"He has no fear...": Muskat, Carrie, "Robin's Return," *USA Today's Baseball Weekly,* August 5, 1997.

"I was not very good...": Hammond, Richard, "Ventura Happy to Let 0.00 ERA Rest," [Los Angeles] *Daily News,* June 26, 2004.

"I knew my ankle...": Associated Press, appeared on ESPN.com, October 11, 2004.

"Ventura was perhaps...": Van Dyck, Dave, "Ventura True Sox Legend."

"I will always feel like...": Van Dyck, Dave, "Ventura True Sox Legend."

Chapter 13

Bo Knows Baseball

"Ordinary people...": Verducci, Tom, "Hip, Hip Hooray," *Sports Illustrated,* April 19, 1993.

"When I don't have to...": Unbylined, "Q&A Bo Jackson," *The Sporting News,* August 12, 1991.

"Right now...": Associated Press, "Bo Signs with White Sox," *New York Post,* April 4, 1991.

Making Beautiful Music

"I've been psychocompetitive...": Ladewski, Paul, "The Ace Is Wild," *Inside Sports,* March 1994.

"That's probably one of the funnest parts...": Rosenbloom, Steve, "Out Loud," *Chicago Tribune,* April 19, 2004.

"Last time...": Rosenbloom, Steve, "Out Loud," *Chicago Tribune,* April 19, 2004.

"I'd rather have a Cy Young...": Rosenbloom, Steve, "Out Loud," *Chicago Tribune,* April 19, 2004.

Comiskey I and Comiskey II

"I really hate...": Castle, George, "Comiskey Is Closed, But 80 Years of Memories Linger," *Baseball Bulletin,* Fall 1990.

Chapter 14

The Big Hurt

"The MVP is something special...": Antonen, Mel, "Thomas' Blasts Outdistance Belle in Home Run Derby," *USA Today,* July 11, 1995.

"We had some fun and that's...": Antonen, Mel, "Thomas' Blasts Outdistance Belle in Home Run Derby," *USA Today,* July 11, 1995.

"If Babe Ruth...": Holtzman, Jerome, "Big Hurt on Horizon; No 3rd MVP for Thomas," *Chicago Tribune,* September 17, 1995.

"I don't know...": Holtzman, Jerome, "Big Hurt on Horizon; No 3rd MVP for Thomas," *Chicago Tribune,* September 17, 1995.

"You can't compare...": Nightengale, Bob, "Jackson helps push Thomas' Attempt to Improve On Subpar 1998," *USA Today Baseball Weekly,* April 7–13, 1999.

Fleet-Footed Luis

"That would take...": Munzel, Edgar, "2,000 Hits for Looey, Still a ChiSox Pillar," *The Sporting News,* May 31, 1969.

"Especially Sherman...": Vanderberg, Bob, "Modest Start to Hall of Fame Story," *Chicago Tribune,* April 16, 2006.

"I see this little guy...": Vanderberg, Bob, "Modest Start to Hall of Fame Story," *Chicago Tribune,* April 16, 2006.

"Nineteen-fifty-nine...": Munzel, Edgar, "Little Looie Sees ChiSox Grabbing Division Crown," *The Sporting News,* April 19, 1969.

Chapter 15

"It doesn't matter…": Ginnetti, Toni, "Unveiling of Statue Brings Out Emotion in Tough-As-Nails Fisk," *Chicago Sun-Times,* August 8, 2005.

"I think getting this…": Mayo, Jonathan, "Waiting His Turn" (Major League Baseball, posted June 30, 2000); www.MajorLeagueBaseball.com.

"I never sought…": Mayo, Jonathan, "Waiting His Turn" (Major League Baseball, posted June 30, 2000); www.MajorLeagueBaseball.com.

"I'm not sure if…": Ginnetti, Toni, "Unveiling of Statue Brings Out Emotion in Tough-As-Nails Fisk," *Chicago Sun-Times,* August 8, 2005.

Chapter 16

Four of a Kind

"I didn't know if…": Padilla, Doug, "Sox Pull Out A Blum," *Chicago Sun-Times Special World Series Section,* November 4, 2005.

"I said, 'Hey…'": Padilla, Doug, "Jenks Off Scott-Free," *Chicago Sun-Times Special World Series Section,* November 4, 2005.

"If I ran for president…": Sullivan, Paul, "Man of the Hour," *Chicago Tribune Special World Series Section,* October 30, 2005.

Stepping Up Big Time

"This is a totally different…": Rosenbloom, Steve, "Jermaine Dye, Out Loud," *Chicago Tribune Special World Series Section,* October 30, 2005.

Everyone Loves a Parade

"This is the greatest…": Wang, Andrew, Oscar Avila, and James Janega, "What a Day for a Parade!" *Chicago Tribune,* October 29, 2005.

"After we won...": Isaacson, Melissa, "Million Thanks a Perfect Tonic," *Chicago Tribune,* September 30, 2006.

"Thank you guys...": Wang, Andrew, Oscar Avila, and James Janega, "What a Day for a Parade!" *Chicago Tribune,* October 29, 2005.

"This is absolutely...": Wang, Andrew, Oscar Avila, and James Janega, "What a Day for a Parade!" *Chicago Tribune,* October 29, 2005.